Why Gandhi is Immortal

Chandrakant Wankhade

Translated by Paromita Goswami

INDIA • SINGAPORE • MALAYSIA

ISBN 979-8-89322-669-0

CONTENTS

ACKNOWLEDGEMENT

I heard Chandrakant Wankhade speak on *Gandhi ka Marat Nahi* before I read the book. The Female Education Society, an educational organisation based in Chandrapur, Maharashtra, organised a public lecture on this topic in memory of the Late Adv. Tarachandji Khajanchi in December 2022. Chandrakant Wankhade, a well-known intellectual and activist, was the main speaker, and the grounds of the FES Girls' High School and Junior College were packed to capacity. The speech left a deep impression on many, and people thronged the stall to buy the book. The idea of translating the book into English was first mooted by Adv. Farhat Baig, after this programme, and it was on his insistence that I agreed to give this rather difficult task a try.

Mahatma Gandhi's life and philosophy have been extensively written and commented upon. Every aspect of the Mahatma's political and personal actions has been dissected by a host of critics, beginning with the Mahatma himself. Therefore, one could well wonder what novel information this book had to offer. At Chandrakant Wankhade's lecture, and later while translating the book, I was struck by the extensive research that the author had done in order to build a cogent argument on behalf of the Mahatma.

According to Wankhade, Nathuram Godse's finger was on the trigger, but Mahatma Gandhi's assassination was engineered by a larger, well-planned conspiracy backed by extremist right-wing discourse and organisation. The killers of Mahatma Gandhi, argues Wankhade, are not the only ones who opposed him in his lifetime and their ideological heirs continue to do so to this date. Gandhi has many detractors who critique him through a range of political-ideological lenses. The problem is never with the criticism but with the canards and vicious character assassination that some sections indulge in. This book is a counter-argument to the outright false propaganda, slanderous insinuations, half-truths and malicious allegations that are deployed to attack Mahatma Gandhi.

In spite of countless attempts to render him irrelevant, even today, the Mahatma's ideals of truth, non-violence, and Satyagraha attract generations from all over the world. It is as if, in spite of their best attempts to physically and politically annihilate him, the Mahatma's detractors are themselves vanquished. And thus, the question arises – why does the Mahatma not die? Why is Gandhi immortal? Why does a frail old man prevail over his brutal assassins?

The original in Marathi *Gandhi ka Marat Nahi* was published in 2019 and led to much public discussion and debates. Thereafter, a Hindi translation by Kalpana Shastree *Gandhi Kyon Nahi Marte* was published in 2022 and was equally well-received. I am glad that my efforts at translation will place the book in the hands of English readers.

I am grateful to Chandrakant Wankhade and his partner, Mayatai Wankhade, with whom I enjoyed many insightful discussions in the course of writing this book. I owe much gratitude to Adv. Farhat Baig, who remained wholeheartedly committed to this project from its inception to completion. I would like to thank friends like Adv. Neeraj Khandewale, Adv. Kishore Ram Lambat and others who have supported this book wholeheartedly.

For Kalyan, without whose encouragement and support this book would not have been possible - thank you for having more faith in me than I do in myself.

Chandrapur

1st March 2024   Paromita Goswami

CHAPTER 1

INDIA BEFORE GANDHI

Before the British flag was hoisted over Shanivar Wada in 1818, the Peshwas ruled over Maharashtra. In other States of India, the British captured power from the Rajputs, the Jats and the Muslims - Maharashtra was the only state where power went from the Brahmin Peshwas to the British. Commentators of the time urged the Peshwas, in particular, and the Chitpavan Brahmin community, in general, to overthrow the British and retrieve political power. The general sentiment amongst the Brahmin community time was that since political power had shifted from the hands of the Chitpavan Brahmins into the hands of the British, it was the Chitpavan Brahmins who were destined to retrieve it and enjoy it. In other words, before Gandhi, the implications of political independence were restricted to the retrieval of the 'throne' from the British by the Peshwas.

The sentiments of the Brahmins can be easily exemplified through the article published by *Lokhitavadi* on 1 April 1849. "When will the pleas of the Brahmins reach the ears of the Gods? A learned man (Brahmin) of the bygone age said: Oh, Sir! It was not a minor chaos that Ravana had created! All the Gods were imprisoned, but did Rama not finally win

Lanka from Ravana? Didn't the stones float on water after all? In a similar manner, the British are bound to drown one day, and Dharma shall be re-established. And the Brahmins will be overjoyed." In other words, just as Rama retrieved glory from the chaos unleashed by Ravana, the present day Brahmins, too, were destined to retrieve their glory from the temporary setback caused by British rule.

The logic of the Brahmin elites' claim to power went something like this: the British will eventually lose, and power will revert into the hands of the Brahmins. But why was it desirable that the British relinquish power? - so that it is restored into the hands of the Brahmins. Why should the Brahmins regain power? – in order to establish Dharma's authority. Why should Dharma be established? – so that Brahmins are pleased. In effect, the very reason for independence, according to the Brahminical elites, was to glorify the Brahmins.

This was the social condition before Gandhi entered the freedom movement. At the time of his entrance, there were already shrill debates within the movement over whether social or political independence ought to take precedence. Lokmanya Tilak was a staunch supporter of political independence, while there were others who questioned whether political freedom without social freedoms would have any substantive meaning at all. Often, such ideological positions led to grave confrontations. Agarkar, who advocated social freedom, was viciously called *ganjivaril kutre* – a dog who eats leftovers. If a renowned public leader such as Tilak did not demur from using coarse language against another eminent social reformer, one might well imagine the level to which his followers' vulgarities plunged. We may even wonder whether, in the name of religious conservatism, Tilak was completely trapped by his own followers in the cage of Brahminical conservatism. There were those among his followers who believed that even if there was only one last Hindu left on earth, that person should be a hard-core traditionalist - one who sported a hair knot (*shendi*) and a sacred thread (*janva*).

Such were the social circumstances in which the Brahmins clamoured for the overthrow of British rule and the establishment of *swaraj* or self-rule. Non-Brahmins or Bahujans, by contrast, offered their support to the British. The former put forward the cause of political independence as the reason to disregard the issue of social equality; the latter prioritised social equality to argue that the time was not ripe to demand independence. Over time, it became a set pattern that Brahmins invariably took the lead in politics, while non-Brahmins opposed them with their insistence on social reforms. There was such severe opposition to any talk of social reform in the circle of political elites that people like Shreedhar Vitthal Date sternly warned against the discussion of any social issue in the Congress Sessions. He warned that the introduction of social issues in the agenda would be considered a 'stigma', and he threatened to burn down the stage of the Congress session if it were to become 'polluted' by discussion of social issues. Patriots who claimed they were ready to lay down their lives for the independence of the country went ahead and denounced social reformers like Agarkar and Deoghar as heretics who did not deserve to live.

It is quite understandable that Lokmanya Tilak could not escape the oppressive social milieu of the times. While accepting Tilak's greatness, his contribution to the freedom movement, and the reverence accorded to him as 'the Father of Indian Unrest', we should not forget that his 'casteist' outlook was that of a typical Brahmin. Towards the end of his life on 11 November 1917, he asks in his speech at Athni, 'Do farmers want to pull the plough in the legislature? Do tailors want to work their sewing machines there? And do the traders want to hold up their balances?' While asking these questions, it does not strike him to ask what good the Brahmins will do in the legislature. The speech shows that even Tilak spoke under the influence of the caste-based system that prevailed in the society with its hierarchy, discrimination, untouchability and conceptions of purity and impurity.

Before Lokmanya Tilak, it was Sir Syed Ahmed who used a similar narrative – one that gives startling insight into the thought process of the 19th-century elite, both Hindu and Muslim. In 1888, while speaking before a group of wealthy Muslims, Sir Syed Ahmed said, "It is very necessary that for the Viceroy's Council that the members should be of high social position. I ask you — would our aristocracy like that a man of low caste or insignificant origin, though he be a B.A. or M.A., and have the requisite ability, should be in a position of authority above them and have power in making laws that affect their lives and property? Never! Nobody would like it."

The truth is that certain questions never arose for discussion in the pre-Gandhi phase of the freedom struggle. Questions like for whom was independence intended? Whose rights should be safeguarded in independent India? Who should wield authority? It was presumed that independence was meant for the social and political elites, those who had the inherent birthright to rule based on social status. No one considered the future of Bahujans. No one asked - what about those at the bottom of the social pyramid? What would *swaraj* bring for them?

In Maharashtra, the leadership of various strands of the freedom movement – whether extremist, moderate or revolutionary – remained with the Chitpavan Brahmins. This is quite evident if we go through the list of names of these leaders - whether it is Vasudev Balwant Phadke, who is revered as the first revolutionary or Ranade, Gokhale, Agarkar, Rajwade, Chiplunkar, Tilak, Savarkar, Shivrampant Paranjape or the Chapekar brothers who killed Rand, all these people were Chitpavan Brahmins. Certainly, this is not a coincidence. It was the outcome of the stated principle of the elites: 'Power went to the British from the Chitpavan Brahmins, it should be reclaimed by the Chitpavan Brahmins, and it should be enjoyed by the Chitpavan Brahmins.' Out of the thirty-seven accused in the Jackson assassination case, all were Chitpavan Brahmins except one. This, too, was another outcome of the 'principled' stand taken at that time. After Gandhi entered the freedom movement, these people's fervent opposition to British rule lost its intensity. Those who felt that Gandhi was depriving them of the 'prey in sight' trained their guns at Gandhi instead of the British. All the men accused in Gandhi's assassination case were Chitpavan Brahmins except for one. This, too, was no coincidence.

Maharshi Vitthal Ramji Shinde did not enter the contemporary debates of whether political freedom should take precedence over social freedom or the other way around. He held that both should go hand in hand. He organised the first 'Asprushyata Nivaran Parishad' (Convention for Abolishment of Untouchability) on 24 March 1918 in Mumbai, the first such convention in India. He was desperate that Lokmanya Tilak should attend the convention, but Tilak was reluctant. Vitthal Ramji Shinde took great efforts and finally managed to persuade him. Tilak agreed, but on one condition – he would not represent *Kesari*, his organisation, but instead, he would attend in his personal capacity. Vitthal Ramji Shinde has described the proceedings of the convention in his book *Dharm, Jivan va Tatvadnyan*. Shinde notes that in his keynote speech in the morning Tilak said, "Even in the times of the Peshwas, Brahmins drank the water filled by Shudras in their water bags; if Gods accept untouchability, then I would not accept such a god." Shinde was afraid that the thunderous applause following this speech was going to bring down the mandap. He further said, "However, when I prepared a manifesto for removal of untouchability and approached Lokmanya for his signature, Tilak was extremely reluctant to sign. Once, he came forward, but Dadasaheb Karandikar stopped him. In the end, Lokmanya was pitiful. He put both his hands on my shoulders and pleaded that I should set aside this request till his return from England."

This incident shows that while Tilak was prepared to cross the boundaries of caste, his followers pulled him back. Perhaps because of his sympathies, Tilak was derided as the leader of the *telyatambolis*, the social underdogs. Certainly, the orthodox Brahmins did not harbour any kind of feelings towards Tilak. According to Damodar Hari Chafekar, Tilak was 'neither a complete reformer nor a complete conservative.' Tilak appears caught in a bind. He comes across as aware of the need to extend himself in order to expand the freedom struggle, and yet, at the same time, he is bothered by the fear of losing followers. Tilak's followers were his strength, but they were also his weakness.

Against the background of the *Vedokta* versus *Puranokta* controversy, Shahu Maharaj expressed his anguish before Prabodhankar Thackeray, "Whether it is Tilak or Gokhale, the patriotism under Brahim leadership has only one reserved compartment. They don't want anyone to touch that." In my opinion, in subsequent times, Gandhi showed courage in touching what Shahu Maharaj called 'the reserved compartment.' Certainly, according to the caste supremacists, Gandhi has repeatedly committed this terrible 'sin.'

★ ★ ★

CHAPTER 2

MAKING OF THE MAHATMA

It is said that the future of great men can be foretold in their childhood. However, such an assessment would not hold true in Gandhi's case. His childhood did not provide the slightest indication of his future greatness. There is no note of his having shown even a glimmer of his extraordinary intelligence in his childhood, nor is there even a faint indication of his extraordinary leadership quality. He did not leave any mark in sports or oratory during his school days. There is nothing outstanding in his academic performance. The score in matriculation is a bare 39%, which is rather average. In other areas, too, Mohandas was no 'braveheart' but quite a coward - scared of the dark, frightened of snakes and ghosts. His childhood friend Sheikh Mahtab encouraged him to eat meat in order to make him a 'strong man', and so Gandhi hid from his family and tried out some non-vegetarian food.

Till twenty-seven years of age, Mohandas Karamchand Gandhi was 'common' and average. Whoever said that the future greatness of a man could be predicted in his childhood had not met Gandhi!

I remember once seeing a film about the devil. The birth of the devil is carefully prepared for in hell. The womb is selected for the devil to take birth in. Advance preparations are made for the protection and rearing of the devil on Earth. The dog of the house in which the devil is to give birth is killed and replaced by a hound from hell to take care of the devil-child. The nurse who is appointed to take care of the new arrival is killed and replaced by a nurse from the devil's quarters. Overall, the denizens of hell plan meticulously in order to prepare for the birth of the devil on earth, for the selection of the house, his future care and protection and the creation of favourable conditions. The stage is thoroughly set before the devil makes his entry.

This film made me wonder whether the things that happen in the case of the devil also happen in the case of a Mahatma. Mohandas Karamchand Gandhi, who lived an ordinary life till 27 years of age, comes to be revered as a Mahatma – a great soul. A glance at the journey from Mohandas Karamchand Gandhi to Mahatma Gandhi reveals startling 'coincidences.'

Gandhi's youth was spent abroad for education. As a student, he decided to follow the British culture - their attires, their dance, moving around in suits, boots and coats, allowing a full ten to fifteen minutes before the mirror to accomplish the proper hairstyle, a dandy to the hilt. Amidst all this, he remained true to the promise given to his mother before leaving India – he did not touch meat. What was extraordinary in that?

Born in 1869, the twenty-two-year-old Mohandas Karamchand Gandhi returned to India as a barrister. He enrolled in the Bombay High Court as a lawyer. He struggles to set up practice. Even the practice is not aimed at anything higher than the maintenance of his family and repayment of loans incurred in student days. His practice lags even after a couple of years of struggle, so he shifts the practice to Rajkot. There, too, he struggles tooth and nail, and there, too, he fails miserably. At last, this barrister from England takes up the lowly and secondary work of drafting petitions, but soon, he realises that this work is not available without paying commissions.

His miserable experiences made Gandhi lose interest in the work. Disheartened and dejected, Mohan applied for the post of a teacher in a school that had advertised for the post of an English teacher. He is denied the post. In India, every door was closed on his face. Barrister Gandhi was really at a loss. In 1893, the doors of law practice opened slightly in South Africa. He received a letter from Dada Abdulla and Company, who belonged to Porbandar's Memon trading community, enquiring whether Gandhi would be ready to travel to South Africa. There was a suit involving the company that was pending in court. In that matter, the European lawyer who represented them did not know any other language than English. Dada Abdulla, on the other hand, did not understand his language. The company expected Gandhi to work as a translator between the company and the European lawyer. Yet another lowly and secondary work had come his way. Gandhi had little choice but to immediately agree to the offer.

A question arises – if Gandhi had not gone to South Africa, would he have become 'Mahatma' in India? Could he have held his own against the stalwarts in India? Would he have survived the competition? After all, the oppressive Indian society of the time carried the burden of caste and the hierarchical Varna system, and the powerful men of the times remained under the influence of these prevailing systems - no matter how bold the man, no matter how strong his flight, yet his leap would never extend beyond the bounds of caste and varna. Gandhi studied abroad. He crossed the oceans and was thus considered 'polluted.' Upon his return, Gandhi was forced to give in to the insistence of his caste community and had to undergo purification rituals. Without the South African experience, would Gandhi ever have moved ahead? To what extent could he have sustained himself in the repressive circumstances of Indian society?

The doors of opportunity were closed to Gandhi in India. Helpless and vulnerable, he was forced to go to South Africa. It was here that he was introduced to himself, and from there on, he set out on the path that led to his becoming 'Mahatma.' The conditions were already favourable and nourishing for him in that far-off country. Even before Gandhi's birth, the 'Little India' in South Africa was preparing itself as Gandhi's laboratory. Since 1860, people from different parts of India entered South Africa as labourers and traders. They included Tamil and Telegu-speaking people from South India. There were also Hindi speakers from Bihar and North India. Indians from various castes, religions, languages and states were brought together by providence in South Africa, and together, they formed the Little India for Gandhi. Sometimes, one wonders, was the destiny of Mohandas Karamchand Gandhi becoming Mahatma pre-decided before his birth?

The manner in which the doors in India are closed to Gandhi, his departure for South Africa, his understanding of intense racism in that land and the manner in which circumstances prevent him from slipping back home after his work ends - everything occurs in an astonishing fashion.

Let us take a look at the day which was supposed to be his last day in South Africa. Barrister Gandhi, who landed in South Africa in 1893, is prepared to leave the country at the end of the year. As part of the farewell, Dada Abdulla has invited many important Indians to spend a day with Gandhi at Sydenham on the shores of Natal. There, Gandhi is drawn to a daily news item. The news pertains to a proposed Bill to deprive Indians of voting rights. Naturally, since all important Indians are gathered there, the matter comes up for discussion. In the discussion, Gandhi said it is the first nail being driven into the Indian coffin. The moment Sheth Abdulla asks Gandhi what they should do, one of the guests present there said, 'Gandhi should postpone his departure by a month.' There is a clamour to 'keep Gandhi back, keep him back.' They request him. They also assure him that they would bring their legal cases to him to ensure that his legal practice provides enough for his maintenance.

Gandhi gives in to their persistence and agrees to stay back for the month. He ends up staying there for more than twenty years. He prepares himself there. He is made to prepare himself. Barrister Mohandas Karamchand Gandhi, who is unsuccessful in India, turns out to be a highly successful law practitioner in South Africa, but his journey does not stop there. Unknowingly, this successful barrister embarks on the journey of becoming a 'Mahatma.'

Although there was nothing to predict Gandhi's future greatness, there were a few uncommon moments in his childhood that we may take note of in hindsight. In this thoroughly common man, we catch the slightest glimpse of the uncommon.

A British inspector visits the school when he is in high school. He gives some questions to the students. The teacher observes that Gandhi has written a wrong answer. He signals to Mohandas to copy the correct answer from the student sitting in front. But Mohandas does not do so. The teacher feels that Mohandas may not understand his signal, so he tries to push him with his foot. But still, Gandhi refuses. Indeed, refusing to copy the correct answer even after the teacher asks him to do so is not a common incident. It shows his basic nature of rejecting what is wrong right from childhood.

Gandhi's father was the Dewan of an estate and naturally held a high economic and social position. Once, Gandhi requested that his friend, who was poor, be invited home to share some mango juice. But when food is served, the friend is absent. Gandhi realises that his friend is purposefully not invited because of his poverty. That year, Gandhi completely boycotted his favourite dishes of mangoes and mango juice. This tenacity of childhood is reflected in later years as well. Kasturba's doctor instructed her to forego salt in her diet. Removing salt from food is as good as rendering it tasteless. Kasturba was not ready to listen to her doctor. The doctor, on his part, was trying his best to convince her, but Kasturba was not ready to give in. Gandhi tried to persuade her. Kasturba retorted in irritation and anger,

"It is easy for you to tell others." Gandhi immediately announced his decision to give up salt in his food. Kasturba realised her mistake after Gandhi's decision. She apologised to Gandhi. She requested him to retract. But Gandhi showed the same resolve that he had shown in his childhood.

Mohandas had gone to see a theatre while his father was unwell. He loved the theatre. When he returns, he finds his father writhing in pain. He is filled with remorse that he had left his father in pain for the mere greed of watching a play. He renounced theatre even though he enjoyed it. Gandhi is yet again seen as steadfastly following his resolution.

Gandhi's mother was opposed to his travelling abroad. His mother was afraid that the foreign culture and lifestyle would lead him to consume liquor, eat non-vegetarian food and get into affairs with women. Gandhi reassured her and promised her that none of her fears would ever come true. Following a strict vegetarian diet in England is a great challenge and difficult, but he has fulfilled his promise. It is clear that Gandhi has twin qualities: strong determination and the ability to remain true to his word.

In his later life, he proclaimed 'truth' as God, but the beginnings of this understanding, however blurred they may be, lay in his childhood. The real anxiety and pain that untruth inflicts on him is anything but normal. In his adolescence, he fell into bad company. He was totally under the influence of this company. He ate meat and smoked and stole money to meet the requirements of his new habits. Later, he came to his senses, and he set his course right. That was all. No one was aware of the wrongs that Gandhi committed. No one found out about the theft, nor did anyone catch the thief. Gandhi could have just gotten away with it. No one had identified him with the misdeeds. It would have been quite normal to just keep quiet about the entire affair. But things took a different turn. Although no one had seen Mohan commit the acts, his own eyes had seen them. The agony and remorse make his life intolerable. In the end, he confesses about his misdeeds in a letter to his father. Under normal circumstances, we try to hide our sins under the fear of what effects a confession would have on others and what reactions it would evoke. We try to cover up our mistakes. We expect our father's anger, scolding, even beatings and being thrown out of the house. What would our mother feel if she came to know? How would the family react? Wouldn't I fall in their eyes? These are the questions which force us to hide our mistakes. But the man who thinks that it is far more acceptable to fall in others' eyes than in one's own and who therefore confesses is certainly not an ordinary person; rather, he is 'extraordinary.' This 'extraordinariness' has been evident since Gandhi's childhood.

The days of his father were drawing to an end. He served his father diligently. But on the night his father died, lustful thoughts of intercourse with his wife preoccupied his mind even as he served his father. He entered Kasturba's room to fulfil his desires, and that very night, his father expired. He suffered guilt his entire life because of this incident. The suffering was natural, but the courage required to share this extremely personal experience with the world was unnatural. The confession of misdeeds in a letter to his father is the 'shorter version' of his life, while publicly sharing the fact that he was satisfying his lust even as his father was on his deathbed is the 'longer version.' Just as he did not care about the reaction his confession would evoke, there is no evidence of any fear while he publicly confesses to his 'sin.' The childhood episode was comparatively easy. But it is a wonder that he did not consider declaring his lust publicly after being called a 'Mahatma' could have led to serious damage to his reputation as a Mahatma. Great people have spent their entire greatness augmenting their reputations, taking care of their reputations and ensuring that not a scratch touches it, but Gandhi does not seem bothered by such concerns. This appears to be absolutely astonishing. Usually, leaders are extremely conscious of what people think about them because they don't want to lose followers. If followers leave him, how will the leader retain his leadership position? We see this in the case of Tilak, who attends the first Asprushyata Nivaran Parishad on the invitation of Maharshi Vitthal Ramoi Shinde, and yet he refuses to sign the public memorandum because Dadasaheb Karandikar stops him from doing so. Tilak gave in to the demands of his followers, not wanting to anger him. Gandhi, by contrast, is never seen bogged down by the consideration of provoking resentment or antipathy in his followers. He does not seem caught up in maintaining his self-image. At the age of 37, he decides to become a celibate and, in his usual manner, follows the decision with tenacity. At the ages of 65 and 67, he ejaculates. Hardly would anyone else even think of sharing this personal detail, but Gandhi, even after he had been called a 'Mahatma', spoke about it publicly and wrote articles about it. He warns the public that even though they might consider him a 'Mahatma', he is not released from feelings of lust. Here, too, it is his own conscience that pricks him. He feels that if he does not confess this failing publicly, it would amount to deceiving the public. The seed of confession that he had planted in his childhood through the letter to his father takes the shape of a large tree in his later years. It does not matter whether anyone else detects one's faults or not; whether they overlook the fault or not, one should not overlook one's own mistakes. Gandhi took a step further and made it a point to bring his faults before the public. The man who is extremely tolerant of the mistakes of others is equally harsh towards his own shortcomings. Usually, people are quick to judge the mote in the eye of others without looking at the beam on their own. It is just the reverse in the case of Gandhi. He would make molehills of mountain-like mistakes of others and present his own smallest shortcoming as a major failing. It is quite evident that Gandhi believed that covering up one's mistakes encouraged the 'thief' inside to become the 'tyrant' ruling one's soul. Gandhi remained committed his entire life to the truth contained in Saint Tukaram's abhang *'satya-asatyashi man kele gwahi, maniyle nahi bahumata'* – one's soul is the witness to truth and falsehood, (it) did not listen to the myriad worldly interpretations.

Gandhi had experienced violence at close quarters during his stay in South Africa, in the Boer War and the Zulu Rebellion. He had seen the great tortures inflicted by the Whites on the Blacks even as he cleaned bullet wounds and bandaged whiplashed bodies. He develops a hatred for such 'manly' violence. He connects all this violence with 'sex' and, therefore, decides to pledge celibacy at the age of 37 years. He decides that only those whose souls are pure are truly strong. He opines that only a Brahmachari who gives up sexual pleasures and is freed of greed can control violence. This is why he sees the partition of the country, which follows the independence of the country, the violence that is unleashed and the terrible bloodshed as a result of his personal failure to maintain Brahmacharya. There can be a huge debate on this issue, and we are free to participate in such debates.

His friends conveyed grave disagreements and discomfort about his experiments with Brahmacharya during the Noakhali riots. Nobody has any doubts about the truth element in Gandhi's 'experiments.' There is no objection to his conducting such experiments. The opposition is to the manner in which these are conducted publicly. Gandhi wanted to do everything in public, while his followers wanted him to conduct the experiments in private. His friends were disturbed that, given the poisonous atmosphere of the days, his experiments would be misinterpreted and misunderstood by people at large, but Gandhi had no such fears. He is neither concerned about his image nor what people would say about him. Even today, the Hindutvawadis deride him in filthy, poisonous and bitter language for his experiments. They use the most unpalatable language for Gandhi, but they forgeot to ask what would have been the case if Gandhi had not divulged these facts. In his childhood, the fear of outcomes did not stop Gandhi from revealing the truth to his father, and in his adulthood, he did not hide anything from the public. At the very least, we have to appreciate the openness and honesty which he displays.

Gandhi never allowed himself to be trapped in the cage of his own image. The anxiety of hurting his image did not stop him from making confessions. This was the nature of his confession in his childhood. In fact, the manner in which he constantly tried to free himself from the 'Mahatmahood' that people bestowed on him, putting himself to the harshest test, begs to be studied separately.

Gandhi was an iconoclast who attacked his own image again and again, and it is a wonder that people still hold him in the deepest reverence. He never bothered that his image as the follower of non-violence would come in the way of his position regarding non-vegetarianism. He did not take up the naïve stance against killing animals to strengthen his image of a pacifist, nor did he bother that his positive stance regarding Indians joining the military would be construed as being contrary to his professed non-violence. Gandhi was never under the pressure of what people would say if he changed a position that he had previously taken on an issue. Many people were shocked when Gandhi took the position that if Pakistan continued to behave in a hostile manner, there would be no alternative other than war. But Gandhi did not stop to take their reactions into consideration. In the end, Gandhi remained free of the trap of maintaining a positive public image or reputation, and therefore there, nothing could hinder his spontaneity.

CHAPTER 3

A STORM NAMED GANDHI

The Gandhi who returned to India from South Africa in 1915 was not the Gandhi who had left the country. The Gandhi who had gone to South Africa was completely demoralised, bereft of hope or self-confidence, helpless and lost. The Gandhi who returned was successful, brimming with confidence. The unimpressive Gandhi had now returned to India as an impressive man. The Gandhi who had left for South Africa did not know himself. Not only did the Gandhi who returned know himself, but the world that did not know the 'old' Gandhi had started recognising the 'new' one. Gandhi had undergone a transformation that was reflected not only in his physical gait, mannerisms and attitude but also in his attire. The Gandhi, who had left the shores of India in a European costume, returned wearing traditional Kathiawadi clothes.

Gandhi considered Gokhale to be his political teacher. In Maharashtra, Gokhale and Tilak were bitter political opponents. Gokhale was a moderate, and Tilak an extremist. Thus, it was only to be expected that Gandhi's arrival in India would invite speculations about whether he belonged to the moderate camp or the extremist one. Tilak's opinion in this regard is of great importance. 'He follows a different path altogether,' was Tilak's assessment of Gandhi. Whatever the opinion of Tilak, his followers treated Gandhi as an opponent based on the simplistic equation that he was Gokhale's disciple. Unfortunately, even Gokhale's followers did not accept Gandhi. Gokhale wanted Gandhi to work in his 'Servants of Society', and Gandhi too harboured a desire to work in this organisation, but Gokhale's disciples ensured that this shared wish would never come true.

It is also true that in Maharashtra, where Varna-based domination and caste-based discrimination reigned supreme, Gandhi's low caste was an obstacle in his path like a cat that gets in the way to trip one over. The basic principle of politics in Maharashtra was quite clear - since Chitpavan Brahmins had lost power, they should reclaim it and enjoy it. This political formulation did not have any place for Gandhi's low caste, and therefore, Gandhi finding a place in the region's politics was quite out of the question.

Gandhi refused to be pulled into the debate of whether political freedom should precede social freedom or the other way around – he belonged to both sides. He was not ready to accept that freedom could be compartmentalised in this fashion. Thus, those who favoured political freedom became his sworn enemies because he supported social freedom, and those who favoured social freedoms distanced themselves from him because he championed political freedom with fervour.

In the pre-Gandhi era, politics in India revolved mainly around the three metropolitan centres of Bombay, Calcutta and Madras, and there were some stirrings of political awareness in cities such as Delhi, Allahabad, Pune and Lahore. Gandhi's politics in India did not begin in any of these urban centres but in the rural areas such as Champaran. He brought to the fore farmers who were exploited by landlords. Bihar was a backward region, and Champaran was the back of beyond. On top of that, Gandhi chose the most backward section of society – the farmers. Through his actions, Gandhi took politics out of the clutches of the upper caste metropolitan sections and into the homes of the most marginalised.

Gandhi was present at the Congress session in Lahore in 1916 when he tried to bring together the moderates and the extremists. Dr Rajendra Prasad writes about this session in his book, saying that it was perhaps the first instance when the Congress session heard a farmer narrate the woes of the farming community. He further notes that Gandhi had encouraged farmer Rajkumar Shukla from Champaran to share the problems of indigo farmers in the Lucknow session.

The resentment of the upper caste and upper class against Gandhi was quite natural given that their singular belief that independence was meant for the happiness of Brahmins was in direct contrast to Gandhi's declaration that 'the aim of independence is to ensure the happiness of the common man, the farmer and the peasants.' Naturally, those who declared that they would burn down the stage if Congress allowed social issues to contaminate the demand for political independence were outraged by Gandhi's open support for the non-Brahmin commoners after the return of Gandhi social issues like the removal of untouchability were being openly discussed in Congress forums leading to resentment amongst the upper castes particularly the Brahmins. Gandhi's explosive statement that he would not be satisfied till the daughter of the Chamar or Bhangi caste occupied the highest office, and in fact, *that* was his definition of independence, created immense uproar. Those who believed and openly stated that 'the British will leave and we will rule' came to consider Gandhi to be their enemy. They found Gandhi's linking of independence with democracy and the announcement that 'in a democracy, the farmer should be the leader' utterly intolerable.

The first major controversy occurred soon after Gandhi's return to Kochrab Ashram. Gandhi had allowed an untouchable couple to live in the ashram, which created a storm not only in the ashram but also in the neighbourhood and across Ahmedabad. Maganlal and his wife left the ashram on this issue. Kasturba, too, was on the verge of leaving. Donors to the ashram threatened Gandhi that they would stop financial support unless he threw the untouchable couple out. Gandhi ignored the opposition posed by his family, friends and outsiders and insisted that the couple would remain in the ashram. He announced that all those who wanted to leave the ashram were welcome to leave, and all those who wanted to stop making donations may do so, but the couple would stay where they were.

One should not compare two persons, but the difference between Gandhi and Tilak with regard to social issues is simply too glaring to avoid. In the debate between political freedom and social freedom, Tilak was clearly on the side of the former and against the latter. Gandhi, on the other hand, pursued political freedom but remained committed to social freedom. Although Tilak attended the convention against untouchability out of respect for the organisers, he ended up refusing to sign the public memorandum condemning untouchability. Gandhi, on the other hand, does not bow before the pressure to get rid of the untouchable couple in the Kochrab Ashram. He does not care about the disagreement shown by his followers, nor does he allow the threats of the donors to sway him. One has to note this obvious difference between Lokmanya Tilak and Mahatma Gandhi on the issue of untouchability. Gandhi faced the greatest animosity, jealousy, hatred and humiliation in Maharashtra and mostly in Pune because of his stance on hard social issues, which eventually led to his assassination. This is the true reason behind his assassination, notwithstanding whatever reasons are offered by the assassins.

The controversy at Kochrab Ashram was followed by the storm at the Banaras Hindu University. The speech delivered by Gandhi on 4 February 1916 on the occasion of the inauguration of the university was volatile, to say the least. Gokhale had asked Gandhi to keep his eyes and ears open but maintain a period of silence, and this period of silence was at its end. Banaras Hindu University was the fruit of Pandit Madanmohan Malviya's labours. Annie Besant had also contributed to its formation. Princes and the landed gentry were present in large numbers at the inauguration ceremony. They had donated large sums to the university. Gandhi first attacked the English-educated class present there and then turned to the bejewelled Rajas, the gentry and other honoured guests in the audience. Gandhi openly criticised them by pointing out that their jewellery from head to toe was acquired through the exploitation of the peasants and denounced them then and there. He said, "Our salvation can only come through the farmer. Neither the lawyers, nor the doctors, nor the rich landlords are going to secure it." The audience was thunderstruck. There was an attempt to stop Gandhi and conclude the programme, but Gandhi continued. Around this time, there had been an attack on Lord Hardinge, and security arrangements had increased. Gandhi observed that rather than living in such high security, Lord Hardinge would be better off dead. "Is it not better that even Lord Hardinge should die than accept a death-like life?" he asked.

There were attempts to stop Gandhi's speech, which did not succeed, and in fact, no attempts to stop him ever succeeded. The message of the programme reached every corner of India. It was a message that Gandhi was here to break through the upper caste and upper-class elitism and made politics a part of the lives of farmers, peasants and the common people.

In effect, Gandhi asked and answered the question, 'For whom is independence? Not just for the high born but for the country's commoners.' Even on the day Gandhi made the speech, it was clear that Gandhi would follow the path of freedom for the very last person, and for that reason, the fanatics would unleash their fury on Gandhi.

Perhaps no other person has faced the kind of contradictory accusations that were heaped on Gandhi. All his life, the Hindutvawadis reproached him for being pro-Muslim. Yet, at the same time, the Muslim League indicted him for being anti-Muslim and pro-Hindus. How was it possible that the same man was anti-Hindu for the Hindutvawadis and anti-Muslim for the Muslims? After his assassination, the Kapur Commission seized posters in the princely state of Alwar, which said that the body of Mahatma Gandhi should be cut into pieces and fed to crows and dogs. The Prime Minister of Alwar was Dr N.B. Khare, a leader of the Hindu Mahasabha, who had declared Gandhi an incarnation of Aurangzeb. According to Khare, the Muslim Aurangzeb could not destroy the Hindus, and therefore, he had taken rebirth in the form of the Hindu Gandhi. It was hardly a coincidence that posters demanding that Gandhi be cut into pieces were put up in a state where an anti-Gandhi person like Dr. N.B. Khare ruled. The extreme hatred for Gandhi manifested in the desire for his body to be vivisected rose from the belief that his love for Muslims had led to the destruction of Hindus. And what did the Muslims feel for Gandhi? Z.A. Suleri was a Muslim League leader close to Jinnah. He wrote in his book 'My Leader' that Gandhi wanted to destroy the Muslims by "absorbing them into Hindudom."

While Hindutvawadis declared Gandhi to be pro-Muslim, the Muslim followers of Jinnah, who did not feel threatened by Hindu leaders like Tilak or Savarkar, felt threatened by Gandhi. They accused Gandhi of de-Islamisation of Muslims. They objected to the pathans donning the Gandhi cap and khadi clothes and accepting the non-violent creed. They further said that Sir Syed Ahmed Khan had tried to stop the destruction of Muslims, but Gandhi did not allow Sir Syed's work to proceed. After the uprising of 1857, the British murdered Muslims in large numbers, but during the Khilafat movement, Gandhi murdered the souls of the Muslims. In sum, Gandhi had converted the Muslims. According to Z.M. Seluri, without Jinnah, the Muslim boat would have been tossed asunder in the waves of Gandhism.

On the one hand, the Hinduvawadis insisted that Gandhi appeased the Muslims and therefore appeased Jinnah, yet in 1845, Jinnah expressed to Barrister Yahya Bakhiyar that if at all he was afraid of anyone, it was Gandhi.

How could Gandhi be pro-Muslim for the Hinduvawadis and pro-Hindus for the Muslims at the same time? How was it possible that a person who was rebuked by Muslims for the 'Hinduisation' of Muslims was also considered by Hindutvawadis as the avatar of Aurangzeb working for the destruction of Hindus?

Further, the imperialists considered Gandhi as their enemy number one, and at the same time, the communists derided him as an agent of the imperialist. For Dadasaheb Khaparde, the staunch follower of Lokmanya Tilak, Gandhi was a spy planted by the British. Thus, the same Gandhi is the enemy number one for the British, a British agent for the communists and a British spy for the Hindutvawadis. Gandhi is an extreme liberal for the conservative forces, and the liberals label him as regressive. The revolutionaries find Gandhi too moderate, while Annie Besant considers Gandhi not just a destructive force but a total anarchist. Some find Gandhi's thoughts rather obscure,, while others find him a heavyweight with ultra-progressive ideals.

Gandhi is a Mahatma (great soul) for some and a Mohatma (greedy soul) for others. He is a saint for some, a wily politician for others, a patriot for some, a traitor for others. Gandhi has empowered people, say some; Gandhi has disempowered people, say others. Gandhi led this country to freedom, say some; Gandhi led to the dismemberment of this country, say others. Politicians considered him a saint who unnecessarily brought spirituality into politics, thereby creating complete disarray. Religious people considered him a politician wearing the armour of spiritualism. Some kept him at a distance because of his religious bent of mind; others rued that had drowned religion in politics.

The first biographer of Gandhi, the Christian missionary Joseph Doke, wrote in 1909, "I question whether any system of religion can absolutely hold him. His views are too closely allied to Christianity to be entirely Hindu; and too deeply saturated with Hinduism to be called Christian…"

One thing appears to be clear: Gandhi cannot be put into a 'rigid framework', and this is the source of the troubles faced by his contemporaries who wanted to 'rule' society. They tried to box Gandhi into the constructs of religion and failed; they tried to fit him into structures outside of religion and failed yet again. He could not be contained in the frames of caste or country. It was equally problematic to categorise him as a politician. Gandhi appears to be a saint but does not fit into that category either. Those who have the tendency to accept what fits into a familiar category rejected him because he remained a misfit.

The theosophist Annie Besant belonged to the mystic tradition, which did not appeal to rationalists. However, the lady's followers considered Gandhi to be truly mystical. On top of that, Gandhi did not relegate his mysticism to religion and spirituality; instead, he dragged it into political matters. Given that Gandhi was considered esoteric by the proclaimed esoteric people, it indicates that Gandhi must have been a huge 'mystery' for everybody.

The further mystery was that the common people stood firmly behind such a man. A human sea followed Gandhi around while his opponents were left high and dry. This phenomenon was inexplicable.

Critics who claimed that "Gandhi has magic but lacked logic" too were impressed by him. Great minds were flustered in the attempt to unravel the mystery behind the magic and exhausted themselves in the pursuit.

Truly speaking, the story of 'an elephant and four blind men' suits Gandhi perfectly. Some considered Gandhi, a naïve simpleton who had landed up in politics entirely by mistake. Another set believed that the sooner Gandhi stopped his interference in politics, the better it would be for both Gandhi and politics, and a third group saw him as the diplomat to beat all diplomats, a politician cunning to the hilt.

Who was the real Gandhi? If at all Gandhi was anything – he was pro-people. Gandhi did not believe in the categories of caste, religion, language, region, or country – he went beyond all such categories and loved people.

The historian T.S. Shejwalkar was a Hindutvawadi who had publicly suggested that Sawarkar should be made the President of Congress. Yet, he was scathing in his criticism of the historical analysis put forward by Sawarkar and Hindu Mahasabha. According to him, "the researcher is Brahmin, the historiographer and analyst are Brahmins, the subject revolves around the pride in Brahmin Raj, the editor is Brahmin, the teacher is Brahmin, the orator is Brahmin, the movement led by them and the audience is Brahmin – reader and followers are Brahmin as well. The negative fallout of this set-up is that great efforts have been put into blowing the achievements of Brahmins from Gaga Bhatt to Golwalkar out of proportion, embellished, falsified and therefore rendered untrue."

The eminent historian Itihasacharya Rajwade proclaimed, "The Peshwas lost power means Chitpavan Brahmins lost power, and therefore they should retrieve it from the clutches of the British and they alone should enjoy it," and Sawarkar tries to re-write history in accordance to this proclamation. What Shejwalkar said about this is equally important, "The manner in which Rajwade has indulged in self-gratification and literary hyperboles by announcing '*bhatkulpatshahi*' (empire of the Bhat clan) and '*brahminkulbadshahi*' (empire of the Brahmin clan) has misled the younger generation of Brahmins in Maharashtra who are going around with bruised knees. The intellectuals of RSS and Hindu Mahasabha have spread the disaster far and wide. That which has never occurred was announced by them as having taken place, and if anyone spoke out against such announcement, their voice was drowned in the cacophonic noise of drums - the false history is successfully installed as truth."

If we investigate the context of T.S. Shejwalkar's observations, it becomes clear that Brahmins were clever enough to magnify the importance of their puny people and downplay the important contributions of non-Brahmins. The greatest victim of such terrible tactics is Gandhi. The man who was followed by the country and who was bestowed recognition internationally was declared a traitor by them – they spun tall tales about how he destroyed the country, how he disempowered the people of the country, how he led to the dismemberment of the country, how he was the cause of Hindu devastation, how the Muslims became insolent through his support, how he placed the interests of Muslims above those of Hindus. The Hindutvawadi camp painted Gandhi's image as a confused, ignorant, foolish person, and he was also presented as a 'deceitful schemer' at other times. Sawarkar's brother Babarao Sawarkar calls him a 'traitor' and a 'great sinner.' According to Vinayak Damodar Sawarkar himself, "Gandhi is the moderate of the moderates and most helpless of the helpless." According to Tilak's disciple Khaparde, Gandhi is evil, shrewd, cunning, a fraud and a spy of the British government. Dadasaheb Khaparde compares Gandhi to a dormant volcano and said of his popularity, "A volcano cannot be recognised till it explodes and therefore till then the donkeys and monkeys dance on its body without suspicion and run around spitting and shitting on it."

Detractors of Gandhi tried to draw his insistence on non-violence in their chorus of support for violent uprisings: "Who can imagine achieving independence without a battle?" The slogan of the freedom struggle under Gandhi was "We shall claim *swarajya* by spinning the *charkha*", which his opponents twisted to "We shall claim *swarajya* by chewing toothpicks." Bhopatkar, the author of *Bhala*, considered himself a 'fervent' yet 'dull' disciple of Tilak and a self-declared vicious opponent of Gandhi. In Maharashtra, he dedicated himself to bitter and acidic remarks against Gandhi. This *Bhalakar* Bhopatkar was one of the creators of the 'chewing toothpick' comment and the labeller of the Mahatma as 'Mohatma' – a deluded soul.

The tales of Bhopatkar are quite scandalous. He used to refer to *Varnabhed* - a difference in the four varnas as *varan bhed*, which could mean either a difference in marriage or a difference in lentils. He argued much in accordance with his fervent and dull nature, "Where is caste difference in the Hindu religion? The four-fold *Varna* system is in accordance with nature. Varna is not colour, but lentils are used in food. Brahmins eat cooked *turi*, Vaishyas *moong* and Shudras *urad*. Thus, the *varans* or lentils are different for each." As soon as Gandhi led the Salt Satyagraha, he immediately started playing the old tune "Who can win freedom without a battle?" and listed out several questions: "Gandhi has conducted the Salt Satyagraha today, tomorrow he will do Satyagraha for turmeric and day after for chilli. Does anyone get independence by doing Satyagraha of turmeric, chilli and salt?"

Gandhi provided human beings with a creative, civilised and cultured tool of collective struggle, namely 'Satyagraha.' Yet, Satyagraha, an important contribution to Gandhi's intellect, was reduced to an object of derision and ridicule by his opponents. Gandhi alone brought various caste communities of India close together, as no other leader had ever done before him and drew hateful malice from those whose arrogance rose out of feelings of caste domination and caste supremacy.

Those who believed that political independence took priority over social independence and who had joined the freedom struggle under Tilak started to withdraw from the independence movement. Others became indifferent. Yet another group considered it a sign of courage to oppose the freedom struggle because they believed that Gandhi's concept of freedom was 'impure.' They held that Gandhi, who belonged to a lower caste, had defiled the freedom struggle by bringing social issues into it. Instead of committing the 'sin' of supporting such a freedom struggle, it was better to earn 'religious merit' by opposing it, and to that end, the Rashtriya Swayamsevak Sangh was founded.

The shift of leadership after Tilak's death to Gandhi in 1920, the introduction of a resolution stating 'untouchability is a taint on Hindu religion' in the Nagpur Congress session of 1920 and the passing of this resolution - all these events were an eye-sore for those who considered the Congress to be a mere political organisation. The formation of RSS within four years of the Nagpur session cannot be seen as a mere coincidence. Those who were horrified to see that Gandhi was using the freedom struggle to attack caste supremacy and caste hegemony went on to form the Rashtriya Swayamsewak Sangh.

Tilak died at midnight on July 31 1920, and Gandhi started the non-cooperative movement on August 1. We don't know whether this is a coincidence. As soon as Gandhi comes to know Tilak's demise, he rushes towards Sardar's house. A lot of discussion had already taken place about Tilak's funeral rites and rituals. Lokmanya's body was brought down. Gandhi moved ahead. Somebody stopped him, saying, "You are not a Brahmin, so do not touch the bier.' Gandhi stops short; he is agitated. He lowers his head and thinks for a while and, with some determination, goes ahead to carry the bier on his shoulder and said to the person who had stopped him, "I don't think a public servant belongs to any particular caste," and thus he became a pallbearer.

Gandhi's actions thus far would have been acceptable. After all, he was a Hindu, even though he was not a Brahmin – the fanatics might have persuaded themselves. But Gandhi does not stop here. He fetches Shaukat Ali by his hand and asks him to shoulder Tilak's bier. From his perspective, when Gandhi became a pallbearer, Tilak went beyond caste, and when Shaukat Ali became a pallbearer, Tilak moved beyond religion. But this action is considered a defilement of Tilak's bier, and Gandhi is held responsible by the fanatics. These religious 'leaders' went on to heap scorn, hate, malice and ridicule on Gandhi, planting the seeds of his assassination.

The Hindu caste system relegated the Shudras and Atishudras to the lowest rung, condemned to perform menial tasks to serve the higher castes. They were expected to perform manual labour and physical work hard. According to the principle of karma, they were being punished for the sins of their past lives by being born as shudra in this life. Thus, if they wanted to make something of this life, they were expected to serve the higher castes without compensation. Just as there was a hundred per cent reservation for Brahmins in the study of Vedas, there was a hundred per cent reservation for the Shudra-Atishudras in manual labour. The question about their place in society never came up in the discussion of the elite Brahmin 'patriots' who wanted India to be independent. Apparently, the miserable lives of Shudras-Atishudras did not concern them at all. They could not be bothered about the question of the dignity of the Shudra-Atishudras and certainly not about their rights as human beings. These things were out of the question with regard to those whose touch was considered polluting. Even their shadow was impure. The products created through their labour were not impure, of course. The food grains they produced did not defile those who ate them. They constructed temples that were not defiled by their touch during construction, but once the deity was installed, they were not allowed to enter. Their entrance defiled not just the temple but even the Gods, and so they were denied temple entry. Their touch defiled the water in public taps. Under the Peshwa regime, the Shudra-Atishudras were made to walk on the roads with brooms tied to the waist and pots hanging from their necks. The broom swept clean the road made unclean by their footsteps, and they spat in the pots hanging from their necks lest their spit makes the surroundings unclean. Therefore, they were not allowed to step out in the evenings when the shadows lengthened, lest their unclean shadows fall on an upper caste and defile them. The Peshwas who had heaped such ignominy on the Shudra-Atishudras lost power to the British in 1818, and immediately, they raised a hue and cry. The loss of the Peshwa's political power had put Dharma in danger. The Brahmins grieved, and the freedom struggle was the only way for them to come out of their sorrow and reclaim their power. As long as Tilak was at the helm of affairs, things were moving according to their plans, but the meddlesome Mohandas Karamchand Gandhi unleashed havoc after the death of Tilak.

In 1916, at the Lucknow session of Congress, an ordinary farmer stood on the dais and narrated his sad plight, all at the behest of Gandhi. The elite leaders were shocked - wasn't the farmer a shudra? How did he reach the dais of the Congress?

Around 1917-18, the same Mohandas Karamchand Gandhi announced that he would not be satisfied till the daughter of *a chambhar* or a *bhangi* did not sit at the highest office of India. This was even more shocking. In fact, according to Gandhi, the very definition of independence was the elevation of a lower caste woman to the highest office. Such statements were traumatic for those who considered the Shudras, who should remain under our heels and seek to be placed on our heads.

The Congress session at Nagpur in 1920 proved to be a milestone of sorts. This session was the last straw on the back of the camel for the faction, which considered that social issues should be kept at a distance from the Congress's political platform. In this session, Gandhi moved a resolution stating untouchability to be a blot on Hinduism, and the resolution was passed. Further, Gandhi stated that those who do not perform bread labour do not have the right to food – 'No labour, no meal.' According to him, those who live off the labour of others are thieves, while those who live by the sweat of their brow are the true rulers of the earth.

Through this talk of the dignity of labour, Gandhi sought to completely topple the existing social structures. He gives dignity to the Shudras and Atishudras and denounces those who do not live off their own labour, who claim status and rights based on birth as 'thieves.' It is unfortunate for the Mahatma that many of those for whom he makes these efforts do not recognise his radicalism. Gandhi believed in class equality. It is often stressed strongly that Gandhi believed in a 'change of heart' and avoided direct confrontations, yet this does not explain why Gandhi's entire life was spent amidst conflicts.

There is no way for us to recognise Gandhi as a radical revolutionary; at the same time, we cannot forget that he maintained open channels of communication with his bitter opponents, even in the middle of confrontations.

Gandhi insisted on bread labour – no one was exempt. He said, 'The lawyer's work has as much value as the barber's inasmuch as all have the same right of earning their livelihood from their work.' Further, 'intellectual work is important and has an undoubted place in the scheme of life. But what I insist on is the necessity of physical labour. No man, I claim, ought to be free from that obligation. It will serve to improve even the quality of his intellectual output.' He insists that in ancient times, Brahmins performed both intellectual and manual labour, and even if they didn't, in the present times, the need for physical labour is self-evident.

Gandhi said all this and that too in the midst of the fight for independence from British colonial rule. The elite sections were, of course, not convinced - what has any of this got to do with independence? Their only objective was to overthrow the British Raj and install Brahmin rule in their place. Gandhi had unnecessarily created hurdles in their path to glory by unnecessarily entering into the why and wherefores of independence and also for whom. He wants to provide dignity of labour, or in other words, dreams of according to the highest status to the labourers. He offers the dream of equality to the common person. The status according to birth was sought to be replaced by status according to labour. One question naturally plagued his opponents – would it not be better if Gandhi were removed from this world? It should not surprise us that over time, for some people, getting rid of Gandhi became more important than getting rid of the British.

Gandhi shattered the dream of the 'educated' caste-class section that political power would fall into their laps once the British left. Gandhi pointed out that political freedom was not true freedom. He was convinced and reposed faith in his understanding that true freedom would mean freedom of the labourers, the workers, the farmers, and the very last person in the country, and he took every step in that direction. According to Gandhi, the very meaning of 'freedom' was that the Shudras and Atishudras who did not have status, who labour and yet did not enjoy the fruits of their labour and who were deprived of their humanity should get social status, respect, value and dignity.

When the issue of voting rights came up for discussion, the elites insisted that education, property and social status should be taken into consideration when deciding on a franchise. Who were these educated people? Who was well off? Those who had education as well as property also had social status, and naturally, these were the upper caste-upper class people. It was very evident that if the right to vote was given according to these criteria, then it would remain limited to the elite (Abhijan) class, and the masses (Bahujans) would be deprived of their democratic rights. The upper caste would use their franchise to establish their authoritarian rule. Against this background, when Gandhi took the strong and insistent view that the right to vote should be given to those who performed bread labour, it led to obvious anger among the upper caste. Gandhi introduced a resolution in the Congress session at Belgaum that bread labour should be the basis of voting rights in Congress. It is a separate matter that the resolution was defeated.

According to Gandhi, it is an indignity to accept assistance of any sort without labouring for it. "My ahimsa would not tolerate the idea of giving a free meal to a healthy person who has not worked for it in some honest way," he said. It is an indication of moral turpitude if healthy persons live as parasites on unearned wealth. Gandhi's efforts were directed at ensuring the dignity of labour to those who were deprived of it and also at demolishing the pride and arrogance of the privileged class. Gandhi identified himself with the common people through his simple living. Further, through his work as a scavenger, he identified himself completely with the untouchables.

Every time he was asked to identify himself in court, he presented himself as a farmer, a weaver, a labourer. He never identified himself as a 'barrister.' Gandhi did not only work for the dignity of the untouchables; his aim was to identify himself with them.

Gandhi's stress on bread labour was not based on morality alone; rather, it had economic, social, and political facets as well. The four-fold caste system had denigrated the labourers as 'untouchables.' Therefore, he placed great stress on bread labour, dignity of labour and faith in labour as part of social and political justice for the untouchables. He tried to establish the charkha as a symbol of the synergy between the labour force in the country and the capital available in it.

Gandhi's opponents have argued against his so-called 'anti-technology' stance. They have deliberately perpetrated a misunderstanding that he is against technology and development. Gandhi, on the contrary, insisted that the use of technology should take into account the needs of the person at the bottom of the social ladder. His insistence was for the judicious use of machines and technology. Those who love India and humanity at large could well ask, "What practical resources and methods can we bring together to combat the terrible poverty and destitution?" The answer to this question will lead them to understand that big industries lead to the concentration of production and distribution of wealth in a few hands, which in turn leads to the creation of privileges and authoritarian tendencies in society, which were abhorred by Gandhi. For him, the choice lay between 'mass production' on the one hand and 'production by the masses' on the other. The question he posed at that time remains relevant to this date. Indian reality today is a painful paradox – on the one hand, the country is on the way to becoming a superpower, and on the other hand, farmer suicides are on the rise; the GDP is rising on the one hand, and unemployment is rising on the other. Is it not true that the godowns in the country are overflowing with grains, and yet children are dying of malnutrition in Adivasi areas? Capital investments are on the rise, but if labour is not equally invested, then should one consider breaking them or providing work to their hands? Aren't these questions posed by Gandhi relevant and burning even today?

Gandhi was not anti-development, but he was definitely of the opinion that any relevant model of development could not be imported. The development of any country can be planned only by a proper assessment of its natural resources, geographical extent, and availability of capital and labour. It would not be correct to expect high capital investment in a country which has low capital availability but surplus labour. Gandhi employed charkha and khadi as symbols of this principle. Charkha spinning does not lead to independence, but when thousands spin charkha together, it creates an energy that can be put to use for the cause of independence.

A man once asked Gandhi, "What is the definition of your economics?" Gandhi answered, "To convert waste into wealth is the definition of my economics." Let us consider Gandhi's definition of economics and contemplate what might be considered as 'waste' in the country today. There is fallow land in the country, i.e. wasteland. Rainwater runs off into the sea, which is a waste. Solar energy is going to be wasted, and people are not employed; therefore, their energy is wasted, too. Human minds and bodies are lying useless without contributing to the labour force of the country. To imagine the conversation of such wastes into wealth and to insist that the government should plan towards such wealth creation can hardly be labelled as 'Gandhi's idiocy.' On the contrary, if we look at the contemporary definition of economics, it is really "to convert wealth into waste," and this is the direction of modern development. There is a great contrast between Gandhi's conceptualisation of economics as the conversion of waste into wealth and today's situation of converting wealth into waste. It is a separate matter that we have relegated Gandhi's thoughts on converting waste into gold to the waste bin.

★ ★ ★

CHAPTER 4

GANDHI'S NON-VIOLENCE

'Ahimsa' is an ancient word found in Hindu, Buddhist and Jain philosophies, and it has been stuck to Gandhi. There is an unbreakable connection between Gandhi and 'ahimsa.' But Gandhi was not the only follower of 'ahimsa.' Those who believed that violence was synonymous with courage condemned Gandhi's ahimsa as cowardice. They deployed the word 'ahimsa' as evidence of Gandhi's cowardice, but in reality, no evidence is required to show that Gandhi's ahimsa was far from cowardice. Gandhi experienced bloodshed in the Boer War in South Africa while working in the Ambulance Corps. During the Zulu rebellion, he also experienced the cruelties of war and violence. He must have read or heard about the 1857 War of Independence, otherwise known as the Sepoy Mutiny or Revolt. In 1857, the British army fought against the British and lost the war. In the Boer War and the Zulu Rebellion, Gandhi had a glimpse of the manner in which the British were adept at crushing armed revolts and strengthening their empire, similar to what they had done in 1857. He realised that the usual methods of armed confrontations would be of little use in the struggle for freedom. It was nearly impossible to challenge the empire by killing one or two British people.

Tilak's position was that if there is half a chance of victory through armed revolution, then the other half can be managed, but such revolutions may not be undertaken if the chances of failure are forbiddingly high. Tilak approaches the matter of violence and non-violence not in philosophical terms but as a matter of practical strategy. For Gandhi the matter is philosophical as well as practical. If the nation is to be free, the first question is 'Which nation?' - All that exists is a nation fragmented by caste and community. The member of the British House of Commons, Ramsey MacDonald, writes in his book *The Making of India* that the Brahmins consider India as limited to their caste. In such circumstances, it was important to unify the country and make independence relevant not only to a handful or few people but also to the common people at large. The greatest challenge before Gandhi was to ensure that the hopes and aspirations of the common people were reflected in the independence struggle.

It is true that Gandhi believed in non-violence, but certainly, he was no fool to consider that non-violence would exist alongside exploitative systems. During the First World War, Lokmanya Tilak, Annie Besant and Gandhi were all active. Gandhi was of the opinion that the colonial government should be assisted unconditionally. He wanted the common people to join the army and learn the use of arms. Thus, his ahimsa went hand in hand with public appeals to join the army. It was not just a simple appeal, but he worked day and night to convince his fellow countrymen. It would not surprise anyone if Tilak or Annie Besant would have worked with such passion, but the devotee of ahimsa certainly surprises us in this matter. All three leaders were in favour of the war effort, but Tilak and Annie Besant wanted it to be conditional support; Gandhi alone wanted the support to be unconditional. His argument against Tilak and Besant's stand was that negotiating during the Second World War would be a loss of opportunity for Indians to train in the use of arms. He wrote as much to Pandit Madan Mohan Malviya. In this context, he said that developing physical strength to the full potential was the pre-condition for practising ahimsa.

One may well ask why it was impertinent to join the army and learn modern weaponry. The answer is indicated in a pamphlet issued by Gandhi on 23 June 1918 at Nadiad titled 'Appeal to Enlistment' in which he wrote, "If we want to learn the use of arms with the greatest possible dispatch, it is our duty to enlist ourselves in the army. There can be no friendship between the brave and the effeminate. We are regarded as cowardly people. If we want to become free from that reproach, we should learn the use of arms."

In 1925, Gandhi spoke out against the colonial policy of disarming Indians. He said the British have emasculated the common Indian by taking away their arms. This is a Black Act they committed. He states, "Among the many misdeeds of the British rule in India, history will look upon the Act depriving a whole nation of arms as the blackest." He further states that although he does not believe in an armed revolution and is committed to ahimsa, he would support any campaign initiated against the Colonial Arms Act. Those who declare that independence cannot be achieved without bloodshed are nowhere to be seen when Gandhi said these things. This is because they maintain a careful distance from the freedom struggle led by Gandhi.

In 1918, Gandhi appealed for enlistment and in 1925, he opposed the Arms Act, which was aimed at disarming Indians, and in 1930 he made the important demand to amend the Arms Act in order to allow the licence of arms to citizens for self-protection. This demand is part of his 11-point ultimatum submitted to the Viceroy. This is an important point to note.

Gandhi was a Mahatma, a great soul. He was devoted to ahimsa, and he is the father of our nation. Amidst all these smooth epithets, we forget that he was also the Commander-in-Chief of the national struggle for freedom. He was a courageous veteran.

In the debate between violence and non-violence, he was undoubtedly on the side of non-violence, but this does not mean that he considered those who strove for independence using violent means as 'untouchables.' About the prisoners of the Azad Hind Fauj, he said that though he could not support any violent fight for independence, he could not turn a blind eye to the patriotism of the INA soldiers. Gandhi and Subhash Chandra Bose are sometimes painted as bitter enemies. However, during the final retreat of the Azad Hind Fauj Netaji addressed the INA soldiers, saying that after their return to India, they must become soldiers of peace and work under the directions of Gandhiji. Such facts are always conveniently forgotten by the opponents of Gandhi.

Gandhi knew that India House in London was a nerve centre of militant activities. The strategies were made here, although the bombs exploded elsewhere. Gandhi was aware that Madanlal Dhingra had assassinated Lord Curzon Wyllie in London, and the leads pointed towards India House. India House was put under secret surveillance by the London police. The Indians in London decided to celebrate Dushera in India House in 1909 and to invite an Indian leader for the programme. But no Indian leader was willing to go to the infamous India House. Gandhi gladly accepted the invitation despite knowing the risks involved. His sole condition was that instead of calling for food from a hotel, they should cook food at home. Since all other leaders had refused the invitation, the organisers accepted Gandhi's condition out of fear that he might refuse, too. Gandhi, the chairperson of the function, arrived earlier than expected. He went to the kitchen and asked for some work and happily accepted the task of dicing vegetables. As the time to begin the programme drew near, the organisers, including Sawarkar, were anxious. By chance, one of them entered the kitchen and was shocked to find Gandhi there. The incident shows that Gandhi was willing to enter places that other people found below their dignity. He did not care about what others would think or say. He disliked Madanlal Dhingra's actions but did not comment on them. He publicly appreciated Sawarkar's patriotism, sacrifice and bravery. Gandhi never considered anybody inferior because they followed a different path than his.

Today, some people seek to disgrace Gandhi by committing false accusations against him. They opposed him and also opposed the movement which he led for India's freedom. This opposition is primarily because of Gandhi's insistence that freedom should not be for a handful of elites alone but for the Bahujans as well. He surmises that if Bahujans are to join the freedom struggle, then their dreams, hopes and aspirations should be reflected in the struggle; they, too, should feel that freedom is for them. Once the reins of the struggle were in his hands, Gandhi included the Bahujans in the struggle. He was very clear in his understanding that the participation of Bahujans in the struggle today would open the doors for future participation in governance tomorrow. This is why Gandhi worked hard to include the issues of farmers, workers and women in the freedom struggle. Unfortunately, his honest efforts were not appreciated by those who were gripped by the egoistic beliefs of superiority in the hierarchical Varna system.

Gandhi's elite opponents faced a further problem - how could they openly challenge Gandhi? Open opposition would expose their bigotry, and therefore, they tried to don the mask of 'nationalism.' But this was a poor cover for their real intentions, and they were exposed no matter what they tried. Till today, it is their problem that once their veil of nationalism is ripped away, their Hindutva is exposed, and once the layer of Hindutva is removed, the Brahminical vested interests hidden underneath are bared. Gandhi had created a big problem for them. By saying, 'all those who do not labour are thieves,' he made it quite clear who the thieves were. Gandhi said that thousands of villagers have sacrificed themselves so that 'we the elite' may survive, and now it is time for the elite to make sacrifices so that the villagers can survive. For Gandhi, the prestige of the elite class was created through the deaths of the masses of lower cases, and by saying that the elite should be prepared to die for the subalterns; Gandhi once again disrupted the dynamics of older social relations.

For Gandhi, the work of the lawyer and the barber was of equal importance. He was of the opinion that there is not much difference between intellectual work and that of a conservation worker. In fact, he held that the work of the lawyer is immoral. Dadasaheb Khaperde's response to Gandhi's assessment of lawyers is very telling; he said, "Gandhi has risen against the life and livelihood of Brahmins."

As Gandhi's power grew, the prejudice against Gandhi converted into hatred. Gandhi's increasing power weakened his opponents; they could neither go with Gandhi nor oppose him openly. This led to hopelessness and despair, which fed the hatred, envy and bitterness against Gandhi. Several attempts to assassinate Gandhi failed till the last bid was successful. There were some pitiable attempts to provide reasons for the assassination. The assassins attempted to bury the real reasons under wild accusations and derision. Their mischievous attempts to stigmatise Gandhi continue to date.

We cannot say who coined the phrase '*Majboori ka naam Mahatma Gandhi*', i.e. 'Mahatma Gandhi is the synonym for weakness' – nor can we say from where it arrived. Unfortunately, however, it has taken root and has become almost a truism. The phrase has stuck with Gandhi so much that it is almost impossible to pry it loose today. The country accepted Gandhi's leadership because of his capabilities. At best, we can say that it was the country's helplessness which led it to accept Gandhi's leadership, but how could it be Gandhi's helplessness? And therefore, how can one say 'Gandhi is the name for helplessness'? But it was said and continues to be said. Congress was forced to accept Gandhi's leadership – sometimes willingly and sometimes unwillingly. This was perhaps the helplessness of Congress, but how does it prove that Gandhi was feeble or helpless? Gandhi forced an imperial power like Britain to leave this country. He inspired the common people to fight and perform extraordinary acts of bravery. Gandhi awakened the collective courage in people and defeated the British. Gandhi's tactics were such that often, the British would be in a quandary whether to detain him or let him go. They were unable to make up their minds what to do about him. Where does this show Gandhi's feebleness?

Those who harbour hatred against Gandhi and resent him created the ecosystem for his murder. Some were so joyous at his death that they openly distributed sweets, but over time, if they too are forced to include Gandhi's name in their morning prayers, then whose weakness does it show? Does it show the weakness of Gandhi or his assassins? If the Prime Minister, who is known for his foreign tours, is obliged to the name of Gandhi, then who should be labelled 'weak'? Shouldn't one say *Majboori ka naam Modi* instead of using the words for Gandhi?

Gandhi's statues have been erected all over the world. Postage stamps have been issued in his name. Innumerable books have been written about him. Universities have named Chairs after him. Does all this show their dependence on him or Gandhi's dependence on them?

The truth is that *majbooti ka naam* Gandhi - Gandhi is another name for strength. Gandhi was always strong even though the people whose vested interests were imperilled sought to declare him a weakling.

A canard has been spread about Gandhi, saying that it was he who said, 'If someone strikes me on one cheek, I shall offer the other.' Overall, Gandhi's personality is not such, and yet these sentences were slapped onto him. If we consider the journey of Gandhi in its entirety, then we see that he has taught people to oppose injustice and oppression, not to tolerate injustice. It is a different matter altogether that Gandhi's methods of opposition had no place for hatred. And therefore, it is worth considering why Gandhi would say that if he were struck on one cheek, he would turn the other. In the film *Lage Raho Munnabhai*, these same words were also put into Sanjay

Dutt's mouth. This film was not anti-Gandhi; on the contrary, it was created out of love for Gandhi, in spite of this, the sentence was included.

It is true that this sentence belongs to Gandhi, but the context is entirely unique. Gandhi used this sentence during the Harijan Yatra. The sentence was like this: 'Savarnas have committed so many injustices, oppressions on Harijans that if they strike me on one cheek, I shall turn the other cheek, and yet it shall not be enough to compensate them." But later, people jettisoned the context and started to use the sentence as a stand-alone, and thereafter, it became popular as such. This sentence was used without context as evidence of Gandhi's impotence, weakness, and cowardice – qualities that were never part of Gandhi were thus foisted on him. This sentence was used to show the allegations against Gandhi were an inherent part of his personality; the allegation was deployed purposefully to manufacture the anti-Gandhi narrative till finally, the decontextualised sentence achieved social acceptance as truth and the interpretation as self-evident. This canard shrouded Gandhi's radicalism, his revolutionary philosophy, his rebellion against the established systems, the priority he gave to Bahujans in his activism, and his leadership. Thus, his opponents achieved what they conspired to do, and unfortunately, Gandhi's friends and supporters fell prey to this propaganda as well.

'Gandhi is the name of weakness' is used to paint the picture of Gandhi as feeble, passive and helpless and 'if struck on one cheek I will turn the other' was used to show him as impotent, foolish, meek and cowardly. These sentences are used without their contexts and successfully presented by the rumour-mongers as Gandhian principles, and to top it all, they whisper, "What did Gandhi's goat eat? Nothing except cashews and raisins!"

The narrative of Gandhi's goat feeding on dry fruits was embedded skilfully to belittle the journey of Barrister Mohandas Karamchand Gandhi in his well-cut suits to Mahatma Gandhi in his loincloth. If Gandhi's goat was fed cashews, then it would be rather easy to write off his loincloth, his simplicity, and his hermit-like lifestyle as hypocrisy. In a country where the poor do not have enough to eat, how can anyone accept a so-called messiah of the poor as the Mahatma when he feeds his cashews and raisins? Thus, the seeds of hatred against Gandhi were sown very skilfully, and his supporters were clueless about their opponents' tactics. Even more than Gandhi's words, it was his actions that had a deep impact on Indians. Gandhi not only spoke about simplicity but lived a simple life. Therefore, the accusation that Gandhi fed his goats with expensive dry fruits confused the common people. How can we say that this poisonous propaganda left the Indian people untouched?

Gandhi was extremely careful about public finances. He established the Tolstoy Farm in South Africa. Herman Kollbach bought the eleven acres of land required for the ashram and handed it over to Gandhi. The rule was that ashram dwellers should walk the twenty-one-mile distance to the nearest town, Johannesburg. Many times, there used to be a contest as to who would walk the distance first. Once, Kollenbach wanted to take up this 21-mile challenge. He set his bag on his shoulder and set out quickly. He carried his tiffin in his bag. But in order to win the challenge, he ate from the roadside stall rather than stopping on the way, opening the tiffin and eating from it, and eventually, he won the challenge. When Gandhi came to know of this, he took up the issue. He is upset at the extravagance shown by Kollenbach and scolds him for buying food instead of eating from the tiffin. Even the man who donates land is not exempted from his frugality. So, how can the goat get away with eating dry fruits?

Mahadevbhai Desai was like his son. Gandhi was living in Mani Bhavan in Mumbai. The office of his mouthpiece, 'Bombay Chronicle', was near the Fort area. Gandhi used to write for the newspaper and hand over the articles to Mahadevbhai to take to the office. Mahadevbhai Desai faced hardship while doing this task. Once, he hired a Victoria Buggy for fifty-eight annas and reached Mani Bhavan. Gandhi scolded him roundly for wasting public money.

Mahadevbhai Desai was like a son to Gandhi, but the rules were not different for his own sons either. Once, Gandhi's son came to visit him in the ashram, and Kasturba served him a special meal. She broke the rule that every person in the ashram should eat the same food. Gandhi not only scolded her but also published an article about the incident. Can a person so strong and transparent about public money feed dry fruits to his goat?

It should not surprise us if the Hindutvawadis throw any wild allegations against Gandhi because it was Gandhi who destroyed their stranglehold over national politics. One can understand their indignation with Gandhi well. Their panic that emerges from hopelessness is also understandable. Out of sheer panic, they made the allegation that Gandhi had fed cashews and raisins to his goat. It is not surprising that they set the trap, but it is certainly surprising that well-meaning people stepped into it.

During my incarceration during the emergency, I experienced how Gandhi was deified and vilified at the same time. There were a large number of Rashtriya Swayamsevak Sangh activists with us. In their morning prayers, the name Gandhi was taken along with that of God. Once their morning rites with Gandhi were over, Gandhi became a 'Satan' for them for the rest of the day. In their talks, they constantly questioned what Gandhi had done in the context of the hanging of Shaheed Bhagat Singh, Sukhdev, and Rajguru. And the way they talked, it appeared as if it was not the British government but Gandhi who hanged the three martyrs. Gandhi was presented as the 'executioner' of the revolutionaries.

In reality, the Rashtriya Swayamsevak Sangh is not remotely connected to the freedom struggle, and at best, the relation was limited to opposing the struggle. Shyama Prasad Mukherjee wrote to the British about Gandhi even as the Quit India Movement of 1942 was going on, "Anybody who, during the war, plans to stir up mass feelings, resulting in internal disturbances or insecurity, must be resisted …I am willing to offer you my whole-hearted cooperation…" The entire country was fighting the British under the leadership of Gandhi, except these self-declared 'nationalists' who were helping the British. These are the same set of people who today decide who should be certified as a nationalist and who should be declared anti-national. There is nothing to show they ever harboured any love for Bhagat Singh when the young freedom fighter was alive. In fact, we can contend that love was non-existent because Bhagat Singh and his friends were fighting the British. There is no question of them harbouring any emotional connection with the revolutionaries. On top of that, Bhagat Singh followed the communist ideology. According to Golwalkar Guruji, who considered communists as enemies, Bhagat Sangh would be considered a member of the 'enemy' camp.

The question arises - why have they suddenly found affection for Bhagat Singh and his comrades after independence? The reason is clear. Although Gandhi was killed by the bullet of Nathuram Godse, he is still 'alive' in the minds and hearts of people. Gandhi's opponents feel the need to hide behind Bhagat Singh in order to mount their attacks on Gandhi. To that extent, they pretend affection for Bhagat Singh. This is the reason why they confounded Indian people by constantly harping on the single question of what Gandhi did to revoke the death sentence of Bhagat Singh and his comrades.

Let us consider for a moment that Gandhi did nothing at all. But then what did the RSS, with their professed affection for Bhagat Singh, do to save Bhagat Sangh from the death sentence? History tells us that Bhagat Singh and his comrades were hanged, but the RSS did not utter a single word in protest. There is not a single letter against the hanging written by the Sarsanghchalak to the Viceroy. There is not a single protest action either, not a single public rally or a public demonstration. Forget at the organisational level; we don't find even the activists of RSS protesting against the death sentence at their personal level. History has not noted a single reaction from the RSS to such an important incident. And yet these are the same people who go around asking, 'What did Gandhi do for

Bhagat Singh'? This is a ploy to shoot from Bhagat Singh's shoulder. These are attempts to silence Gandhi, who is already dead.

Another shoulder that is used to fire at Gandhi belongs to Subhash Chandra Bose. It is important to see what Subhash Chandra Bose himself had to say in his book, *The Indian Struggle: 1920 to 1942*. In this book, he writes, "Gandhiji did try his best to save Bhagat Singh." and this, indeed is the truth. One can try to hide the truth in darkness, but the darkness can be dispelled with a single ray of light.

In 1931, the Gandhi-Irwin Pact was signed. According to this pact, there came up the issue of releasing prisoners arrested during the civil disobedience movement. The British were unyielding when it came to those accused of violence, vandalism, and arson and were not willing to even discuss the issue. Yet Gandhi requested for revoking the death sentence announced against Bhagat Singh, Sukhdev and Rajguru. He tried time and again to convince Irwin - not once, not twice; he tried no less than six times to get the sentence revoked. He wrote letters. Irwin was exasperated with Gandhi and asked, "How can you speak on behalf of those involved in violent acts?" Gandhi replied, "Where does the question of violence or nonviolence come up here? I am trying on behalf of brave, courageous patriots ready to die for their country."

Undoubtedly, there were differences between the revolutionaries and Gandhi on the issue of violence, but the picture that RSS wants to paint that they were enemies of each other because of this difference is entirely false. RSS and Hindutvawadis, in general, were opposed to Gandhi's leadership because independence under his independence would destroy their claims of Varna-based dominance. They could neither support Gandhi's leadership nor could they speak out openly against it – this was their main problem. That is why they tried to demoralise the freedom struggle and worked to defame and abuse him. They used the question of what had done Mahatma Gandhi for Bhagat Singh and his comrades to harass Gandhi when he was alive and continued to use it after his death. Now is the time to ask them a question, "What did you do to demand the revocation of Bhagat Singh's death sentence?"

The Hindutvawadis kept away from the actions of Gandhi and Congress and taunted them by asking how freedom was ever possible through Gandhian methods. What is the relationship between untouchability removal and independence? What is the relationship between the broom, cleaning latrines, removing the hide of dead cattle, making leather sandals and independence? What is the relationship between charkha, takli, and khadi and independence? Independence is not remotely connected with nonviolence. They constantly demanded to know, 'Whoever got independence without battles?' They wagged their tongues without lifting a finger to actually do anything.

If anybody asked them questions, they would give the excuse of not having sufficient strength and thereby keep away from fighting the British. Yet, if someone else took up the cudgels, they would beat the drums, saying the action was a victory for their principles and a defeat for Gandhi. There was no relation between Bhagat Singh and the Hindutvawadis. Bhagat Singh was a communist and a harsh critic of their ideology, but they were delighted at how the actions of Bhagat Singh lowered Gandhi's status. What did they do about Bhagat Singh? Did they open their mouth to demand revocation of the death sentence? Protest against the hanging with whatever strength they did have? No! One can understand that attempts lead to failure, but there is nothing to show that these people have ever tried anything. Their sole work is to insist on asking what Gandhi did for Bhagat Singh. These are people who maintained Bhagat Singh at an arm's length in order to remain in the 'good faith' of the British and avoid being blacklisted, but they harped on the question for so long and with such insistence as if Bhagat Singh was a member of their 'camp.' While asking 'what did Gandhi do?' these people forget the tenet of Hindutvawadis by which a person would be considered 'capable' if the person should have intelligence and strength. At other times, they consider Gandhi a persona non grata because, according to them, Gandhi did not possess either intelligence or strength. But when it comes to Bhagat Singh, they put forward the expectation that Gandhi should have done something to revoke the sentence, and thereby, unwittingly, they imbue Gandhi with strength and capability.

What is true of Bhagat Singh is also true in the case of Netaji Subhash Chandra Bose. Those who are opposed to Gandhi are invariably elated when the discussion of the differences in the methods of Gandhi and Bose comes up. They rejoice that, yet again, someone is opposing Gandhi on the issue of nonviolence. They narrate with glee how Gandhi committed injustices on Bose and disallowed him in the most insulting manner from becoming the Congress president. Suddenly, the sympathy for Bose overflows. Well, what is their relationship with Bose? Bose had a strong socialist mindset and upheld secular values throughout his life. The Hindutvawadis totally opposed these very values which Bose espoused. But they are willing to consider Gandhi a friend even if merely for 'show.' They forget that Subhash Chandra Bose had requested an audience with Dr. Hedgewar, which the latter blatantly refused. To remain in the good books of the British and avoid being blacklisted by them required keeping Bose at a distance. It is their 'double game' - refusing to meet Subhash Chandra Bose in order to remain in the good faith of the British and, at the same time, put up a show of sympathy for Bhagat Singh and Subhash Chandra Bose to show before the people that they are the true 'patriots.'

Churchill was totally against the idea of India's freedom, and he wanted to retain India within the empire at any cost. Churchill listed Gandhi as enemy number one. He constantly insults him by calling him the 'naked fakir.' He insulted Gandhi by refusing to accord him respect, which is due to the leader of the national freedom struggle. The same Churchill is praised by Hindutvawadis because, after all, whoever is against Gandhi is their friend. Such is their nationalism and patriotism.

The RSS was inactive in the Quit India Movement of 1942, but later, they became very active when it came to blaming Gandhi for the partition of the country. According to them, not only did Gandhi partition the country, but he also weakened the shattered pieces. Swami Sachidanand of Gujarat levels two charges against Gandhi in his autobiography titled 'Mara Anubhavo' – the first charge is that Gandhi did not understand the importance of the sword and the second, that he did not understand the dangers posed by Islam.

His detractors held Gandhi responsible for the defeat of India in the war against China in 1962. The war took place 14 years after the death of Gandhi, so how could Gandhi be responsible either for the war or for the defeat? Gandhi never said that an army was not required for the defence of the country. In fact, he takes Vallabhbhai Patel to task when Pakistani tribals enter India, and he supports the emergency action of airlifting soldiers to Kashmir. How do we interpret these facts? Gandhi did his best to douse the flames of communal riots across the country by talking to communities, but there is nothing to show that he is opposed to the government's use of police and army to stop the riots. His stand appears to be that he would do his work in his way while the government was free to do its work using other methods. He had declared that defending the weak was the work of the government. It was not as if he expected the police or army to follow nonviolence. With regard to the kirpan that is worn by Sikhs, Gandhi had observed that, undoubtedly, the kirpan is a symbol of strength, but it should be worn only by those with great self-control and the ability to use it as a last resort in a desperate situation. When Gandhi said that the sword should be used legally, with patience, and to defend the weak, then it is clear that he is not against the sword, but he provides guidance as to how the sword is to be used. It is not as if Gandhi does not value the sword, but he is of the opinion that it gains value only when a steadfast and restrained person uses it to protect lives.

One thing about Gandhi is surprising. Those who are cowardly never understood his nonviolence. However, those who were violent or who were violently courageous immediately understood Gandhi's nonviolence. The Pathaans of Peshawar used to be at the forefront of thievery, dacoities, murders, and riots, and yet they and their leader, Khan Abdul Gafar Khan, immediately understood nonviolence. Subhash Chandra Bose, the founder of Azad Hind Fauj, also understood that through Gandhi's nonviolent movement; soldiers were being trained who were ready to lay down their lives for freedom. Lord Mountbatten was in the army before he became the Viceroy. He wrote to Gandhi, "In the Punjab, we have fifty-five thousand soldiers and large-scale rioting on our hands. In Bengal, our forces consist of one man, and there is no rioting. As a serving officer as well as an administrator, I should be allowed to pay my tribute to the one-man boundary force." Mountbatten wrote that when Gandhi's name was proposed as a member of the constituent assembly, there was great spontaneous cheer, and he (Gandhi) should have been present to hear it. An army officer and administrator thus saluted Gandhi's nonviolence. Only those who have used sticks to perform exercises since 1925 make fun of him.

Once, General Cariappa said in a speech in England, "To be counted among the great nations of the world, India needed a strong army and, under the circumstances, nonviolence was of no use." Gandhi took issue with him through the columns of *The Harijan*. Later, when the two met, General Cariappa said, "We soldiers are a much-maligned community. Even you think that we are a very violent tribe. But we are not....Of all the people in this world, the one community which dislikes wars is the soldier community. It is not because of the dangers and horrors on the battlefield, but because of the knowledge we have of the utter futility of wars to settle international disputes. We feel one war merely leads to another. History has taught us this." If the General of the Indian army felt this way, then how different is this from what the General of the Indian freedom struggle felt? He, too, said that hatred creates more hatred, and war leads to another war.

Gandhi said in the prayers of 26 September 1947, "If we were convinced that we could never expect justice at the hands of the Pakistan Government and if they did not admit their mistakes, then we had our own cabinet which included Jawaharlal, Sardar Patel and many other good men. If even they cannot stop the Pakistan Government from indulging in those things, then ultimately, they would have to resort to war. If we want to have justice, let me tell you the matter does not lie with you or me. It is the function of the Government. Tell the Government it is there to help us. We should not take the offensive. But we must be ready to fight because when war comes, it does not come after giving a warning. We should not take any initiative to fight, but if the other side takes the initiative, both governments will face their doom. War is no joke. After all, how long can I go on stressing the point? But if there is no settlement between the two sides, there would be no alternative." This is the stand he took regarding Pakistan when he was alive. Nowhere did he say, "Don't battle with Pakistan," "Do Satyagraha in front of your army," and "Do nonviolent resistance." In spite of this, he was alleged to be a 'pro-Muslim' and 'Pakistan lover.' How can one allege that Gandhi, who was upset at India's inability to deal with Pakistani guerrillas and who supported the emergency deployment of the army to deal with the matter, made India weak?

One and half years before his death, Gandhi was asked, "What would free India look like?" Gandhi answers, "In my India, the first and the last would be equal; in other words, no one would be the first and no one the last." In Gandhi's conceptual world, there would be no 'high' and 'low' castes based on the accident of birth, nor would there be domination based on Varna, and no privileges would accrue on the basis of Varna and Jati. What a sin! How could the one who emerged from the mouth of Brahma be equal to the one who emerged from the feet of Brahma? If all were to be equal, this would mean that a handful of people would lose their special rights. For them, there was nothing to achieve through Gandhi's Swarajya; rather, it meant the loss of everything that they had been born into. That is why they did not want such independence at all. Moreover, they did not want the person who brought about such freedom to remain alive, and they were successful on 30 January 1948.

Gandhi's nonviolence was not the nonviolence of the coward. On the contrary, he held strongly that 'anything is better than cowardice. There is double the violence in cowardice.' In order to clarify his stand, he narrates the story of the Black preacher," the Black preacher was insulted by the Whites in the railway, and he said, 'I am sorry' and left for another compartment. This is not ahimsa. This is contrary to the teachings of Jesus Christ. On the contrary, it would have been much more courageous to oppose the Whites," said Gandhi. In Gandhi's ahimsa, there was no place for cowardice. A fearful hare trying to escape the jaws of the hunting dogs is not particularly ahimsa. The hare is already half-dead and struggling to escape. His desperate struggles increase the hunger of the hunter-dog and increase the violence. Gandhi is ready to accept violence rather than commit cowardice. However, he also holds that nonviolence is hundreds of times better than violence.

The restrained manner in which the Satyagraha peacefully faced police action to take the Dharasana salt pans into control was certainly not cowardice. That single incident shook a country like America and forced the British to negotiate with the volunteers. In the movement to boycott foreign cloth, Shirish Kumar stopped the truck carrying foreign cloth and was martyred; Babu Genu, too, was martyred in the same way; such sacrifice was in no way less than that of the revolutionaries who accepted the death sentence with a smile. Courage is required not just to pick up the gun and kill the opponent but also to face the bullet with restraint and resolve. Gandhi aroused such fearlessness in the common people. He aroused collective courage and valour in them. It is not as easy to encourage collective action as it is to inspire individual acts. The fact that people were ready to die for freedom on a single call from Gandhi is extraordinary, even miraculous.

Gandhi's nonviolence was not the simplistic abhorrence towards killing per se. It was Gandhi who said that rats should be killed because the plague, which caused the death of many, was caused by rats. How many people know that Gandhi had advised nonvegetarians to continue meat eating and not convert to vegetarianism in times of food shortage, although he was himself a staunch vegetarian? He also claims that he has broken neither the principles of ahimsa nor of vegetarianism. According to him, vegetarianism cannot be promoted by force. It can only be promoted through personal examples before meat eaters. Further, according to Gandhi, internal conflicts, exploitation of the poor for the pursuit of wealth and suppression of women are worse than meat eating. If meat eaters keep themselves away from these sins, then they will be the best followers of ahimsa. They are better than vegetarians who harbour all the other sins but are conceited because of their vegetarianism. This shows that Gandhi does not limit himself to surface behaviours, but his fundamental nature is to address the central problems. Vegetarianism and non-vegetarianism do not determine who is a better person, but Gandhi associates superiority with economic exploitation and suppression of women. For ordinary people, it is enough to show superiority when we say that one does not even eat a piece of betel nut, even if the person concerned sucks the blood of the poor or is a known murderer. When we put the moral yardstick at 'he wears the scared beads, he does not each meat, he does not consume alcohol and so much so that he does not even chew betel nut' then the person goes scot-free even if they may well be corrupt and exploitative. Unfortunately, Gandhi's radical side is never discussed.

Gandhi goes to the extent of saying that in certain circumstances, it would be a sin for meat eaters not to consume meat. He said that it is not possible to completely eradicate violence from one's life. The question arises: what are the boundaries between violence and nonviolence? While for Gandhi, meat eating is a sin, he said that those who have always consumed meat and who do not feel there is anything wrong with it should not give it up merely to follow him because that would be a sin. Is there anything more that one could add to what Gandhi said?

Gandhi's nonviolence starts with abhorrence towards animal killing, but under certain circumstances, he allows animal killing. At present, we see the chaos that wildlife lovers are creating – they are fine if human beings are killed, but none should touch an animal. It is acceptable if farmers commit suicide because wildlife destroys their crops, but wildlife should neither die nor be killed. It is fine if people die of snake bites and also if there are no antidotes or doctors in rural areas, but snakes should not be killed. However, Gandhi's perspective in this regard is quite different.

In 1926, Gandhi's friend Ambalal Sarabhai killed sixty stray dogs in his industrial premises. There was a big hue and cry thereafter. But Gandhi supports the action through his *Young India*. In 1928, monkeys destroyed the fruit trees and vegetables in Sabarmati Ashram, and Gandhi himself proposed that the monkeys should be killed, thereby astonishing his disciples. He said that as a farmer, he has to follow the path of least violence in order to protect his crops. Given that the monkeys were destructive, if no other way is left, then they have to be killed. He also said that he would not feel bad if a snake was killed to save a child from being bitten by it. Since he was afraid of snakes, he had no right to expect that others would not be similarly frightened.

A calf in his ashram once fell ill, and the doctors said that he could not be cured. In this case, Gandhi decided that it would be better to put the calf to sleep. When the doctor administers the final injection, Gandhi holds down the calf. Many were upset that the worshipper of ahimsa indulged in cow slaughter, and there was an outrage against Gandhi because of this. A Jain later said that this sin should be removed with Gandhi's blood.

Some have accused him of being pro-Muslim, others of being pro-Hindus, and one feels that he was a pro-human. His being pro-human is difficult for us to digest because we are not used to seeing a human being purely as such. Our eyes are used to seeing caste, creed, religion, language, country, region, gender, race and so on - we cannot love a human being without seeing all this.

Gandhi goes to Noakhali, where he helps the Hindus so the Muslims feel he is pro-Hindu. The same Gandhi goes to riot-torn Bihar, and there, the Hindus feel he is pro-Muslim. For Gandhi, the man dying in Noakhali is a human being as much as the man dying in Bihar; given our prejudices, we find it impossible to accept such clarity. While doing his work, Gandhi challenged deep-seated vested interests, and therefore, his opponents proclaimed that his ahimsa had weakened the country; others were put off by his support of animal slaughter and asked, 'What sort of worshipper of ahimsa is he?.' They are eager to judge him for committing the sin of cow slaughter, for which, according to their traditionalist worldview, the only retribution is to spill his blood.

CHAPTER 5

GANDHI: A HERO OR VILLAIN?

One often feels that while there may be many different heroes from the period of Gandhi, his detractors have reserved the role of villain for Gandhi alone. How can a film or literary work with Tilak or Bhagat Singh, Netaji Subhash Chandra Bose or Dr Babasaheb as the hero be complete without Gandhi as the villain? All are welcome to write and speak freely as they wish against Gandhi; not just this, they are free to blabber anything they want against Gandhi. Nobody burnt the book which described Gandhi as a homosexual, nor did anyone call for its ban. Nathuram, in the play 'Mi Nathuram Boltoy', utters lies against Gandhi, but if anyone dares to point out the truth, immediately the Nathuram supporters bring out the placards of 'personal liberty' from their bundles. One feels a grudging admiration for that boy, Nathuram. One feels like asking how the person who denied Gandhi's right to life is today demanding personal liberty. There was never a riot in this country because Gandhi's statue was desecrated, nor is there any possibility of such a riot in the future. Nobody ever takes offence to how you address Gandhi. Nobody will insist that you address him as Mahatma Gandhi or Rashtrapita Gandhi. Many years ago, there was unrest in Kashmir when the 'Hazratbal' went missing, but not a single word was uttered when Gandhi's spectacles went missing from Sewagram ashram; riots were out of the question. The disinterest in Gandhi is not a mere accident – such disinterest was carefully manufactured and propagated by Hindutvavadi forces.

In 1933, Gandhi took out an extensive Harijan Yatra. He was campaigning hard for Harijans to enter temples. It was but natural that his campaign would draw the wrath of the Sanatanis. A man called Lalnath appeared at every public meeting and hurled abuses at Gandhi. He publicly threatened to stop temple entries. He would try to disturb the meetings. All these activities were done before Gandhi arrived. Lalnath was never sure that he would get an audience, so he satisfied his desire for public leadership by making speeches and hurling abuses against temple entry before the crowds that came to hear Gandhi. Once, he tried to stop Gandhi by lying down in front of Gandhi's car. Another time, he tried to stop Gandhi before the meeting at the place where he was staying. Thrice, the crowds of followers tolerated the disturbances posed by Lalnath; on the fourth occasion, Lalnath and his motley group were given a sound thrashing. Gandhi was not involved in this act of violence, nor had he told people to indulge in such acts. Yet Gandhi took full moral responsibility for this incident and directed his followers to apologise. He, too, apologised through the columns of his newspaper. Things could have stopped here, but Gandhi announced that he would fast for seven days to expiate for the violent act. His followers were unhappy that he would fast for seven days for such a small incident. Gandhi answered, "It is the meaning of democracy that my opponent should have full freedom to speak against me. If somebody stops him from speaking because he is my opponent, then I will fight to death against him." One has to understand that if Gandhi is ready to fight to the death for his opponent's right to oppose, then he is made of a different metal.

It is our experience that no leader is able to move out of the boundaries of the caste community – no matter how progressive his philosophy or how much he tries to free himself from caste distinctions. Shivaji is claimed by the Marathas as their own. Tilak remains the leader of the Brahmins. Mahatma Phule may have spoken out about ending the caste system and establishing the Satyadharma, but he was even relegated to the position of leader of Malis. And do we see anything different in Dr. Babasaheb Ambedkar? But Gandhi is not relegated to any particular caste; he is not claimed by any one particular religion. He does not even remain bound to a particular country. He is truly universal.

Yet, all kinds of allegations are made against Gandhi. Some claim that he propounded the fur-fold Varna system and that he is a casteist. Some claim that he is religious and, therefore, a leader of Hindus. The question is that if indeed Gandhi is so bigoted, how could he overcome the boundaries of caste, religion and country in order to achieve internationalism? How did he escape the iron chains of caste, religion and country? A man who led the freedom struggle of one country should have remained restricted to that one country, but he overcame all such limitations.

It is usually said that tall leaders do not allow younger leaders to grow, just as the shade of the massive banyan tree does not allow smaller plants to grow, and even if a sapling comes up, it remains stunted. However, we do not see this in Gandhi's case. If we take the name of any important leader and try to remember the names of his followers, our list does not go beyond four or five names at best. But we don't face such problems in the case of Gandhi. We can name his followers quite easily, and not just a handful but hundreds and all of them from different walks of life. The question arises – was he not a banyan tree? The answer is that he was not a banyan tree; he was the sky itself. And when has the sky ever stunted the growth of trees?

Whatever the teachings of Gandhi, it is true that the common people were impacted by his assassination, and there were grave reactions. In the beginning, there were rumours that the assassin was a Muslim, but later, the truth came out. It should not surprise us that there was anger against the Brahmins once people came to know that the assassin was a Brahmin. In Maharashtra, the houses of some Brahmins were burnt down in the aftermath of the assassination, although there is no mention that anyone was killed or any woman was molested in this uprising. Nevertheless, whatever happened was unfortunate. Gandhi would not have condoned such acts. If he had been alive, he would have fasted seven days as he had done for Lalnath.

It was Nathuram's choice to kill Gandhi, but what choice did Gandhi have but to die in the hands of Nathuram? And yet, no one holds Nathuram responsible for the arson that occurred and the Brahmin homes that were destroyed. We hardly hear a voice that said if Nathuram Godse had not killed Gandhi, our houses would have remained intact. Yet I have met many people who say that if Gandhi had not died, Brahmin's houses would not have burnt, and thus they hold Gandhi responsible for this violent offence too. What is the reason for this immense hatred for Gandhi? After all, these questions remain to be answered.

The Hindutvavadis and RSS attacked Gandhi by hiding behind revolutionaries, the same revolutionaries whom they long considered 'untouchable.' The RSS was always alert that even the shadow of the revolutionaries should not fall on them in order to remain in the good books of the British and avoid being blacklisted by the colonial masters.

In the Tripura Session of Congress, Netaji Subhash Chandra Bose became the Congress president. He requested an RSS volunteer called Huddar to arrange a meeting with the Sarsanghachalak Hedgewar. Accordingly, Huddar, accompanied by Mr. Saha, one of Bose's assistants, came to Nashik because Hedgewar was living with Babasaheb Raghate in Nashik at that time. Huddar narrates, "Saha waited outside while I went in. The doctor was cheerfully talking with other volunteers. At my request, the volunteers left the room. I told him the reason for the meeting. Netaji is very eager to meet you. He has not told me the reason (why he wants the meeting)."

Dr. Hedgewar told Huddar, "I am very ill, which is why I am coming to Nashik. I cannot even speak." This is the tape he played repeatedly in front of Huddar. Huddar pleaded with him and finally begged him to meet Saha, who was waiting outside, and asked Hedgewar to explain the situation to Saha in order to avoid misunderstandings that he (Huddar) did not want Netaji to meet Hedgewar. Hedgewar immediately lies down and said, "Balaji, I am barely able to speak. Please…"

Balaji Huddar exits the room, and once again, the sound of the cheerful banter between the doctor and his followers reaches his ears.

Mr. M.H. Hatiwalekar, who was a follower and close associate of Sarsanghachalak Dr. Hedgewar, wrote an article titled 'Ek Sahapravas: Sawarkar-Sangh Marxwaad'in the 1991 issue of 'Akshar Vaidarbhi.' In the article, he confirms the account provided by Huddar. He writes in the article how Dr Hedgewar pretends to be ill and refuses to meet the representative of Netaji Subhash Chandra Bose.

N.H., alias Nanaji Palkar, is a strong activist of RSS, and Dr. Hedgewar's biographer writes in 'Dr. Hedgewar Prerak Jeevan Prasang' that Netaji tried twice to meet Hedgewar but failed in both attempts. Although he stops short of saying that Hedgewar avoids the meeting, it is quite clear that every time Netaji Subhash Chandra Bose took the initiative to reach out for a meeting with Dr Hedgewar, it was never the other way around.

The Sarsanghachalak of the Rashtriya Swayamsevak Sangh was not ready to even meet Netaji Subhash Chandra Bose, and yet the same RSS people paint Mahatma Gandhi as a villain who conspired against Netaji Subhash Chandra Bose to remove him from the office of Congress president. Many stories, truths, half-truths, myths, and semi-truths about the relationship between Mahatma Gandhi and Subhash Chandra Bose are grist to the rumour mill. The aim of all these stories is to create disgust and abhorrence against Gandhi in society and also to encourage hatred against him.

Subhash Chandra Bose, who had passed the ICS exam, entered the freedom struggle instead of taking up a well-paying job. He was consumed with the pursuit of freedom by any means. He does not allow the considerations of violence – nonviolence, means-ends, and conscience to come in the way of freedom. Gandhi insists on all these values. There are definitely differences between Mahatma Gandhi and Subhash Chandra Bose, but Mahatma Gandhi loved Netaji like his own son. Their differences did not come from the affectionate relations that both of them shared. During the Congress session at Calcutta, Gandhi fell ill and stayed at Netaji's house, during which time Subhash Babu nursed him.

In the Congress session of 1938, Gandhi proposed the name of Subhash Chandra Bose for the office of president, and the latter was elected as the president. In 1939, a Congress session was held in Tripura, and Gandhi, who was in Rajkot, did not attend this session. In this session, the Congress Working Committee was inclined to elect a new president, whereas Netaji desired to continue as the president. Therefore, in Tripura Congress, there was a face-off between the Congress Working Committee and Netaji. Neither side was ready to compromise. There were reasons for the Congress Working Committee to oppose Subhash Babu. The Congress stand was clearly against Hitler, in spite of which President Subhash Babu had secretly met Hitler in the Taj Mahal Hotel, and this incident was revealed to the Congress Working Committee. Overall, the Congress committee was dissatisfied with Subhash Babu's working style. They were adamant that Subhash Chandra Bose should not get a second term, and elections were in play. Pattabhi Sitaramaiyya was the Congress candidate, and Subhash Babu contested as the rebel candidate. There is no doubt about Subhash Babu's popularity, and therefore, the AICC elected Subhash Babu with majority votes, and the official candidate, Pattabhi Sitaramaiyyah, was defeated.

Gandhi was nowhere in all this, but he did give his reaction, "The defeat of Pattabhi Sitaramaiyyah is my defeat." There was no anger or resentment in this statement against Subhash Babu, but Gandhi's enemies used this sentence to make a mountain out of a molehill.

It is the prerogative of the newly elected president to appoint his cabinet, but the working committee creates hindrances, and the AICC passes a resolution that the executive should be formed under the guidance of Mahatma Gandhi. When Subhash Babu approached Gandhi to seek his help in forming the new body, Gandhi refused, saying that it was the prerogative of the president to appoint the new cabinet and he would not like to meddle in the process.

Netaji Subhash Chandra Bose formed the new executive, but Pandit Jawaharlal Nehru, Vallabhbhai Patel and Rajendra Prasad refused to join. Subhash Babu said, "I do not want to remain the president of a cabinet that does not include Nehru, Patel and Rajendra Prasad." Afterwards, he resigned from the presidency of Congress. Where is Gandhi involved in the entire process? And yet Gandhi is declared a 'villain' by the Hindutvavadis to show Netaji Subhash Chandra Bose as a hero. It would have been acceptable if they did this out of true love for Netaji, but there is nothing beyond blatant malafide use of Gandhi's and Netaji's names.

Around 1939, Gandhi wrote to Subhash Babu in which he described the latter as a lost bird, and if his truth and love were pure, then Subhash Babu would return to the brood. The compassion shown by Mahatma Gandhi in this letter is touching.

Netaji Subhash Chandra Bose founded the Azad Hind Sena and named the platoons of the Army after Gandhi, Nehru and Maulana Azad. The basic answer to those who want to sow antagonism between Gandhi and Bose is that if such antagonistic feelings had existed between the two, Netaji would not have named the platoons of his army after Gandhi and his followers.

Gandhi was detained in the Aga Khan Palace when he was seventy-five years old. Subhash Chandra Bose celebrated Gandhi's seventy-fifth birthday with great fanfare in Singapore along with his army colleagues. Netaji was the first one to address Mahatma Gandhi as the Father of the Nation. While celebrating Gandhi's 75th birthday in Singapore, Netaji said that if Gandhi had not come forward in 1920 with the new weapon of nonviolent Satyagraha, then even today, India would have been on its knees begging mercy before the British. He further describes Gandhi's contribution to the Indian freedom struggle as unparalleled and extraordinary. He said about Gandhi, "No single man could have achieved more in one single lifetime under similar circumstances." According to Subhash Chandra Bose, after 1920, it was because of Gandhi that Indians could learn the meaning of national pride and self-confidence. Thus, one soldier saluted another soldier. Only a soldier can honour a soldier, something that others may not understand.

CHAPTER 6

WAS GANDHI A CASTEIST?

A constant charge against Gandhi is that he is a casteist person. The charge is made by many, such as Arundhati Roy, the well-known writer and leftist ideologue, who made this allegation against Gandhi. If Gandhi is a casteist, then it is difficult to explain many of his stands and actions. After his return from South Africa, Gandhi established an ashram in Kochrab where a couple from the untouchable community came to live. There was an outcry not only in the ashram but in the nearby areas as well. There was pressure from within and outside the ashram that the couple should not be allowed to stay. Prominent donors threatened to stop giving donations to the ashram if the couple did not leave. Close relatives actually left the ashram because of this issue. Not just this, even Kasturba very nearly made up her mind to leave the ashram.

Gandhi remained unmoved under this severe opposition. He said that those who wanted to leave the ashram were free to do so. Those who wanted to stop donations were free to do so as well. However, under no circumstances would the untouchable couple be asked to leave. Gandhi had just returned to India and was yet to settle down properly. Thus, if the ashram had indeed closed down, he would have been rendered homeless, but he was ready to put everything at stake for the untouchable couple. On what basis can this action be labelled 'casteist'?

Even before Gandhi returned, the debate about whether political independence or social freedom took priority had reached a crescendo. The elite position was that the Congress forum would be defiled by social issues, and if at all such issues came up, they threatened to burn down the stage. In spite of this strong opposition, Gandhi proposed the programme of removal of untouchability in the Congress session of 1920 held in Nagpur. Does this show that Gandhi was a casteist? If Gandhi is a casteist, then why did he say publicly in 1918, "The daughter of a chamber and bhangi should sit in the highest position of the country. This is my dream and my definition of swaraj." By making such statements, he invited the hatred of the Hindutvavadis - does this show he is a casteist person?

"Untouchability is not a sanction of religion; it is a device of Satan. The devil has always quoted scriptures... But scriptures cannot transcend reason and truth," Gandhi said, once again inviting the wrath of fundamentalists. Does he do so because he is a casteist?

Gandhi did not consider untouchability to be an integral part of Hinduism and declared that he was ready to give up Hinduism if this were the case. In 1915, he said, "If it were proved to me that untouchability is an essential part of Hinduism, I, for one, would declare myself an open rebel against Hinduism itself." He said, "If I discover that Hindu shastras really countenance untouchability as it is seen today, I will renounce and denounce Hinduism." He declared that he loved the Hindu religion more than his life, and therefore, he felt burdened by the stigma of untouchability. In the above quotes, we don't see Gandhi supporting casteism. There are innumerable instances of Gandhi's inclusiveness, and if people insist on calling him casteist, then there is little one can answer.

After his release from Yerwada jail, Gandhi took out a Harijan Yatra covering 12,500 km. This yatra led to great discomfort and anger amongst the upper caste Hindus. They tried to create hindrances and stop this yatra. In 1934 in the midst of the Harijan yatra, there was a bomb attack on Gandhi. Fortunately, he escaped unhurt. Gandhi tried to remove untouchability; he acted for the entry of Harijans into temples; thus, in the eyes of the right-wing fundamentalists, he was drowning out the Hindu religion, and their wrath led to attempts on his life. This is the reason why he was eventually killed. In spite of this, if he is accused of casteism, then the speaker is committing the worst defamation. The casteist Manuvadi people killed Gandhi because he tried to remove untouchability.

The leftists brought class to the centre of public discourse and refused to acknowledge the centrality of caste in Indian social life. On the other hand, Nehru felt for a long time that Gandhi's insistence on the removal of untouchability diverted attention from the primary goal of political independence. Patel, who was in Pune jail with Gandhi, advised him clearly not to interfere between communities and to allow them to sort out their differences. But Gandhi said that this would amount to betraying thousands of Dalits, and therefore, he refused Patel's advice. Gandhi realised that Dr Babasaheb Ambedkar would not be able to withstand the storms cooked up by the traditionalists, and therefore, he purposefully directed the storms towards himself.

It may be true that Dr Babasaheb accorded the highest importance to the caste issue, and Gandhi did not do so for good reasons. There are differences between the two on the caste issue, and these differences are fundamental. This is because the lines of contest followed by the two are quite distinct. Dr. Babasaheb drew a line between Dalits and Savarnas, whereas for Gandhi, the line was between the imperial British and India. Therefore, Gandhi could never have been as aggressive about the caste issue as Ambedkar. Gandhi wanted the unified strength of the Savarnas and Dalits to fight for independence. He had to keep in mind the independence struggle, which should not suffer, whereas Dr Ambedkar was free of such considerations. It would be an injustice to declare Gandhi a casteist without taking all these things into account. On the one hand, he was fighting the traditionalists; on the other hand, he was fighting for independence against the British; and on the third side, he was putting his life on the line for Hindu-Muslim unity. While conducting these actions, he was worried that the fruits of independence should reach the last person at the bottom of the social pyramid. Gandhi's perspective on untouchability should be evaluated after factoring in all these variables.

It is one hundred per cent true that 'Gandhi believed in a four-fold Varna system', and it is equally false. Let us place the sentence in context. Gandhi had said, "I believe in the Varna system, but in this four-fold Varna, there would be no place for high and low." There has never been a Varna system like this, and Gandhi's sentence is an unreal hypothesis. There is no Varna system without divisions into high and low. Gandhi does not believe in the Varna system, which actually exists, but believes in one that is non-existent. This is not a matter of mere wordplay, but throughout his entire life, Gandhi refused to accept discrimination between high and low. "There should be dignity of labour" means who should have dignity? The people at the bottom of the Varna system, the 'Shudras', should get dignity. In which other expression do we have the dignity of labour and, therefore, the dignity of Shudras? "Those who eat without performing bread labour are thieves" – now who are such people who do not perform bread labour? Those who sit at the top of the Varna hierarchy because of their birth and, therefore, sit on the backs of the other varnas do not need to perform manual labour. They have the sole privilege of pursuing knowledge. This is the section that does not labour and is whom Gandhi calls thieves. Gandhi said that he did not accept that Shudras should be denied the right to learn the Vedas. According to him, knowledge was not the private property of any one class or Varna. These were the beliefs of Gandhi. In spite of this, those who continue to say that Gandhi believed in the Varna system should be condemned as liars.

On studying Gandhi closely, one thing becomes clear: Gandhi was not ready to avoid the 'space' occupied by religion. Whether this is desirable or not is a question which can whip not just a storm but utter chaos. Gandhi wanted to hold fast to this space, but he also wanted to get rid of the fundamentalists who had forcibly encroached into the space of religion. Gandhi said, "I love Hinduism dearer than life itself..." which means that he loves Hindu Dharma but loves it more than life. Thereby, he tries to take the space of religion in his control and in the very next sentence, he said, "the taint (of untouchability) has become for me an intolerable burden", which indicates that those who support untouchability do not love the Hindu religion at all. If they had truly loved the religion, then they, too, would not have tolerated the burden of this blot. Gandhi indicates that he hates the blot of untouchability because he loves the Hindu religion more than his life, while those who accept untouchability do not have the slightest love for the Hindu religion.

"I love Hinduism dearer than life itself" is a sentence Gandhi uses to occupy the space of religion. Alternatively, it is used to throw out those who have forcibly occupied the space of religion. In another sentence, he said, "Untouchability is not a part of Hinduism." One way of interpreting this would be to say that those who practice untouchability cannot be Hindus at all. Once again, he enters the space of religion and dislodges the fundamentalists who claim ownership of that space.

By saying, "untouchability does not have the sanction of religion; it is a device of Satan. The Devil has always quoted scriptures", Gandhi calls out bigots, fundamentalists and dogmatists and also insists that untouchability has nothing to do with religion and is the work of the devil. If anyone tries to support untouchability by quoting scriptures, then Gandhi points out that it is the Devil who quotes the scriptures, and thus, he places those who practice untouchability at the level of Satan. This is something that people ought to understand and appreciate.

Manuvadis declared Gandhi to be a heretic, and they decided to 'slay' him. The ideological opponents of the Manuvadis declared him to be a Manuvadi, a casteist person, a defender of the Varna system – indeed there is no bigger misfortune than this. On the one hand, Gandhi occupied the space of religion, and on the other hand, he started to redefine religion. This is truly a 'sin' according to the Brahminical elites because they alone have the right to interpret religion. The caste-Varna to which Gandhi belongs does not enjoy the right to interpret Dharma. If he is redefining and reinterpreting Dharma, then it is a sin because according to the Varna system, this is an example of *'karmasankar'*, i.e. confounding the occupation and rights that are appointed to each Varna, and such *karmasankar* is punishable by death. Shambhuk had committed the same sin, and therefore, Rama slayed him. Shambhuk was a Shudra who tried to study the Vedas and, therefore, overstepped the boundaries of Dharma. Sant Tukaram, too, had declared 'we alone know the meaning of the Vedas' and thereby overstepped the boundary of *karma* allotted to him by birth and therefore he was punished by 'being sent to Vaikuntha in his own body.' Gandhi transgressed the boundaries of Varna throughout his life, and therefore, the religious bosses decided that he deserved the death sentence.

The traditional Varna system has reserved tasks such as scavenging and removing the hides for the Shudras and Atishudras. But Gandhi made everyone, including Brahmins, perform these tasks as part of his programme of untouchability removal and ensuring dignity of labour. He inspired many savannas to transgress the boundaries of Varna, thereby actively promoting 'karmasankar.' If Gandhi had believed in the Varna system, would he have encouraged such transgressions?

Appasaheb Patwardhan belonged to the high-caste Chittapavan Brahmin community from Konkan. Yet, under the inspiration of Gandhi, he spent his life scavenging and working in leather. People mocked him, saying, "We have heard that Gandhi brings dead people back to life and makes them walk around on their legs, but here he has made a man on two legs walk on all fours like a pig." Appasaheb Patwardhan was only one example. There are innumerable examples of Gandhi encouraging karmasnkar. Under the Varna system, the transgressors of karma deserved to be slain, and therefore, Gandhi deserved to die, didn't he?

Under the Varna system, the 'varnasankar' transgression of Varna is even more sinful than the 'karmasankar' transgression of occupation. Gandhi not only encouraged karmasankar but also openly promoted varnasankar. There is no mercy for varnasankar and certainly no mercy for those who promote it. Gandhi set out to remain present in marriage ceremonies, but later, he made the decision that he would not remain present in marriages where both the bride and groom were from the same caste. But if the marriage was between a savarna (upper caste) and dalit (harijan, according to Gandhi), then he would make sure to remain present. This was the revolt Gandhi had against the Varna system and his open promotion of Varna transgression. Gandhi was so strong about this decision that it hurt his family as well. The marriage of Gandhi's close associate Mahadev Desai's son was organised. Gandhi considered the groom Narayan Desai, his grandson, but he did not attend this marriage because it was between two people of the same caste. Mahadev Desai tried to convince him, as did others, but without success. Gandhi said, "For once, there can be an exception for others, but how can I make an exception for a son of my own family?"

Gandhi, who promoted transgressions of karma and Varna, was better recognised by his enemies, but his friends refused to recognise his true worth. By repeating ad nauseum that 'Gandhi is a casteist and Gandhi believes in the Varna system' and they end up directly and indirectly helping the real casteists and Manuvadis.

Gandhi and Ambedkar

Gandhi was opposed to separate electorates, for which he fasted in the Yerwada jail. He created pressure on Ambedkar, who was forced to accept the 'Pune Pact.' Through the Pune Pact, Gandhi deprived the untouchables of their rights, which appeared to be well within their reach. To this date, Dalits have not forgotten this 'wicked' act of Gandhi, and it does not appear as if they will forget it in the future.

But let us examine whether it was wickedness on the part of Gandhi to put his life at risk and oppose separate electorates for the Dalits. Rather, it was the need for the freedom struggle to unite people from all castes, creeds and religions. It was the policy of the British to pick holes in the united front that the leaders wove. Every time the Indian leadership tried to form a united front, the British would pull it asunder. It was only natural for the British to plan every move and strategise to destroy every united effort. The British were not going to serve independence as a golden platter to the Indians. When Hindus and Muslims tried coming together, the British responded by creating separate electorates for the Muslims thereby planting the seeds of partition. The Lucknow Pact, created under the leadership of Lokmanya Tilak, only watered this seed.

The separate electorate, which was created for the Muslims in 1909, was later announced for the Dalits in 1932. Mahatma Gandhi used the weapon of fasting against it because he wanted to defeat the British ploy of creating rifts in the Indian freedom struggle. Many times, there is confusion between reservations and separate electorates. Gandhi's opposition to a separate electorate is interpreted as his opposition to reservations. While opposing separate electorates, Gandhi clearly said that double the number of seats that are reserved for Dalits, but he would oppose separate electorates even if it led to his death.

There was a great commotion at that time because of Gandhi's decision to go on a fast. Undoubtedly, the fast created pressures and tension on Ambedkar. He was also under the pressure of the country-wide support that Gandhi received. But the fast created far more pressure on the traditionalists. One day before the fast began, a resolution was passed in the Sanatani Hindu Sabha, "amongst Hindus, no one shall be regarded as an untouchable by reason of his birth and those who have been so regarded hitherto will have the same rights as the other Hindus in regard to the use of public wells, public roads and other public institutions." Gandhi's fast led to immense social churning. A disease like untouchability cannot be removed by laws alone, but a change in people's mindsets is required. The process of change in mindsets began definitely through this fasting. Overnight, the doors of temples were opened for the untouchables, and the traditional obstructions and regulations were set aside. In city after city, inter-dining between Brahmins and non-Brahmins started. Many felt that they were seeing the disposal of the social filth which had stagnated in Indian society over centuries. Rabindranath Tagore felt that he was seeing a miracle occurring before his eyes.

Overall, the fasting was against the divide-and-rule policy of the British; it was also an attempt to provoke the conscience of the Hindus. If Hindus were not ready to remove untouchability, Gandhi was ready for his life. In the letters written a day before the fast, on the morning of the fast, he writes that his death should not be mourned if he dies in the course of the fast. In the letter written to Miraben, he writes that no pain is too great to bear for washing away the sin of untouchability.

Gandhi's fast presented three questions. Would the Hindus of India remove untouchability to save his life? If they did so, would Dr. Babasaheb Ambedkar moderate his stand? Would a change in Babasaheb's stand lead to MacDonald's reconsideration of his award of a separate electorate? The answer to all three questions was largely positive, and therefore, Gandhi's fast came to an end. Gandhi's life was saved, and people heaved a sigh of relief.

After signing the pact (the Pune Pact) Dr. Babasaheb Ambedkar said, 'I was astounded to see that the man who held such divergent views from mine at the Round Table Conference came immediately to my rescue and not to the rescue of the other side.' Gandhi and Ambedkar had differences of opinion. The lines of battles were drawn differently for the two, and therefore, such differences were quite natural. In the first Round Table Conference, Dr. Babasaheb Ambedkar attacked Gandhi strongly. He used the strongest words to criticise Gandhi. But Gandhi replied, Thank you Babasaheb. Thank you." Gandhi thanked Ambedkar and said, "He (Ambedkar) has a right even to spit on me, as every untouchable has." This was not a superficial stand because he put his life at stake to remove the stigma of untouchability and did not maintain any negative feelings towards Babasaheb. Once Dr. Babasaheb Ambedkar remarked about this to Gandhi, "You understand me and my views, but not your followers." If Dr. Babasaheb Ambedkar would have been alive today the people like me would have definitely said to him, "Babasaheb, you understand Gandhi and his views to the extent that your followers do not."

Pandit Nehru created the first national cabinet and showed the list of ministers to Gandhi. Gandhi saw the list and asked whether the list was for the national cabinet or for the Congress cabinet. Nehru was confused at this question, "What is wrong?" he asked.

Gandhi answered, "Why is Babasaheb Ambedkar's name not on the list?"

Nehru was surprised at Gandhi's question. He said, "Dr. Ambedkar is an opponent of Congress. How can he be included in the cabinet?"

Gandhi repeated his question, "Are you making the Congress cabinet or the national cabinet?" Nehru was speechless, and Dr Ambedkar was included in the cabinet. Only a person whom people called Mahatma, or Father of the Nation, could do this, and he did it. Gandhi was not hindered by Ambedkar's severe opposition to him, and that is why he is called Mahatma.

Another incident of a similar nature. The discussions for creating India's Constitution were going on. Who would draft the Constitution, how would it be drafted, and should foreign experts be called in as consultants? Should foreign consultants be contracted for the task? Gandhi intervened in the discussion between Nehru, Sarojini Naidu and others.

"Why? Do we not have expert consultants in our country?"

"Who is there?" asked Sarojini Naidu.

Gandhi answers, "Dr. Babasaheb Ambedkar."

Thus, Dr. Babasaheb Ambedkar was included in the constituent assembly. Today Dr. Babasaheb Ambedkar is recognised and praised as the creator of the Indian Constitution. But what if he would not have been given this opportunity at all? Thus, it would be ungrateful to forget the role played by Gandhi in that context.

Mahadev Desai's son Narayan Desai has narrated a touching incident in his book 'Adnyat Gandhi.' He writes in his book, after Gandhi's death, an incident occurred. Gandhi's secretary Pyarelal was going towards the Khadi Bhandar of Connaught Place in New Delhi. Suddenly, a car stopped near him. A man in a suit got out of the car. Greeting Pyarelal, he handed over an invitation. The person giving the invitation was Dr. Babasaheb Ambedkar. It was the invitation of his second marriage. His marriage was fixed with a Brahmin lady. Dr. Babasaheb Ambedkar handed over the invitation card to Pyarelal and said, "If Bapu would have been alive today, he would have been happy."

Babasaheb had made this remark because he probably remembered that Gandhi would only attend inter-caste weddings and avoid weddings in which the couple were from the same caste. There were many differences of opinion between Gandhi and Ambedkar, but there was no personal enmity – as is clear from this incident.

However, the unfortunate hatred that Ambedkarites harbour towards Gandhi can be quite perturbing. This does not hurt Gandhi in any way at all because he has moved way beyond such calculations of gain and loss. However, this definitely harms the progressive movement for socio-political change. The intense anti-Gandhi sentiments of Ambedkarites, in effect, strengthen the Manuvadis against whom there is a need for concerted opposition. It is a simple question. How can the same Gandhi, who is the enemy number one of the Nathuram supporters and Manuvadis, also be the enemy of the Ambedkarites, who consider Manuvadis to be their prime opponents? Is it only because of the Pune Pact? How can Gandhi be the enemy of a pact that Babasaheb accepted? One can understand that Gandhi cannot be their 'friend', but how can he top the list of their 'enemies'? Gandhi is considered an enemy by Nathuram; if so, how can the same Gandhi be treated as an enemy by the anti-Manuvadi stalwarts like Kanshiram and other Amberkarite leaders? One can presume that something is seriously wrong and perplexing. It has become extremely important to clarify matters in the present times of rising frenzy. The ideologies of Gandhi and Ambedkar are supportive of each other and not contradictory to each other.

CHAPTER 7

GANDHI AND RELIGION

Gandhi returned to India from South Africa and toured India according to Gokhale's instructions. He went to the hut of Mahatma Munshiram near the Himalayas. There, a strong adherent of Hinduism requested Gandhi to bear the marks of Hinduism on his body. Gandhi refused to wear the sacred thread because the lower castes had no right to wear it. But he agreed to keep the tuft of hair at the back of his head according to Hindu traditions. Later in life, he removed that tuft as well. But this does not mean that he let go of Hinduism entirely – in fact, he held on to Hinduism tight with both hands. Perhaps he understood that in order to fill the space of religion, it was important to hold on to the tail. This is why we see Ram in Gandhi's life; we see Ram Naam and the chanting of the names of Ram. But there is no temple dedicated to Ram on his ashram premises, and we don't even see a photograph of Ram. Gandhi believed in God but never visited a temple to worship a deity. Not only did he not visit temples outside, he also did not allow a shrine inside his Ashram. Prayer is an integral part of Gandhi's life, and a prayer hall would have been expected in the ashram, but Gandhi does not allow that either. He does not allow any believer to construct such temples and shrines inside the ashram. There is God but no temple. There is no temple and, therefore, no idol, and because there is no idol, there is no question of ritualistic prayers. And yet the same man, while writing from Yerwada jail, writes 'Yerwada Mandir' at the top of his correspondence. Does it mean that he considers and converts the prison into a temple? One can't say. Where do God, Ishwar, and Parmeshwar reside for this man? Sometimes, Gandhi provides us with the address. 'I recognise no God except the God that is to be found in the hearts of the dumb millions. They do not recognise His presence; I do. And I worship the God that is Truth or Truth which is God, through service of these millions." Thus, he traps both – the believers in God as well as the non-believers. When he indicates that God is not in temples, then he creates difficulties for those who make a 'business' of religion. He creates philosophical difficulties for non-believers as well. It is difficult to categorise Gandhi as a theist and equally difficult to categorise him as an atheist.

Only Gandhi knows how many people he baffled in the name of God and religion. No one else created as much perplexity in the world of God and religion as Gandhi did.

To begin with, Gandhi inverted the definition of God. It used to be a truism that 'God is truth', but Gandhi inverted it into 'truth is God.' Since he inverted the definition of God, the other religious conceptualisations could not escape untouched. Gandhi defined Hinduism by saying,

'Truth is my religion, and *ahimsa* is the only way of its realisation.' Gandhi's faith is in 'truth and non-violence', and to search for truth tirelessly is religion or Dharma. In Gandhi's vision, God is truth and love. God is righteous conduct and morality. Bravery is God. Conscience is God, and service to the community and public is service to God. None of this talk by Gandhi about God and religion sounds religious at all. Gandhi said, "I am a Sanatana Hindu," and follows that by saying, "but I don't believe in the authority of the Vedas."' One who does not believe in the Vedas is not a Hindu, and yet Gandhi said, 'I am a Sanatani Hindu.' This Sanatani Hindu issues an open challenge to the Shankaracharya. He said, "No matter what the present Shankaracharya preaches as the true definition of Hinduism, I reject any religious doctrine that does not appeal to reason and is in conflict with morality. I tolerate unreasonable religious sentiment when it is not immoral." He claims to have faith in Hindu scriptures, but in the very next breath, he said that it is not mandatory to accept everything written therein. One question that he poses about the Vedanta is not only piercing and painful; it causes much heartburn for the conservatives. He said, "If Brahmins consider themselves as priests because they have studied the Vedas, then Max Mueller, who has studied the Vedas, could be considered a priest as well." This 'religious' man also said, "To the millions who have to go without two meals a day… God can only appear as bread."

Gandhi fully knew that he would have to occupy the 'space' of religion in order to challenge the terrible exploitative practices and superstitions that went by the name of 'religion', the inhuman customs and traditions, untouchability and the rampant class discrimination. The *Sant Parampara* across the country shows a similar understanding. Even as he attacked the hypocrisy that existed in the name of religion, Sant Tukaram held on to 'Vitthal.' Another saint called Sant Gadge Maharaj used strong words to attack religiosity, saying, "Even dogs lift their legs and urinate on your Gods." And yet Gadge Baba did not give up 'Gopala.' Tukaram Maharaj said in one of his *abhangs*, "Speak as if there is a God, but know in your heart that there is no God," and yet he does not give up Vitthal. Gandhi, too, held on to Ram. He does not let go of the tail of religion, insisting, "I am a Sanatani Hindu."

There are ancient philosophical traditions of *Neti-Neti*' denial' in India, which include the method of denying by occupying the centre, not attacking from the periphery. This tradition was certainly followed by the Bhakti movement and the Sant Parampara. Here, the attempt is to reform from within, offer new meanings, and recreate contexts while claiming to be a part of the 'tradition.' It appears that Gandhi is practising this form of philosophical 'denial' – he avoids saying that he is an atheist because that would open him to criticism not only from the fundamentalist sections but also from ordinary people who would say, 'Since you do not believe in god and religion, you have no right to comment on our religious faith and practices.' It is fine if you say 'religion is the opium of the masses', but then what right do you have to speak about our religion at all? Have you converted to another religion? Then what right do you have to talk about our religion? It is only when Gadge Maharaj chants' Gopala Gopala Devakinandan Gopala' that the common people are ready to accept the harshest criticism of religious practices from him. The religious sentiments of the common people are not hurt when he attacks their practices. But if the same harsh sentiments are expressed by those who claim that there is no God, then it would not be tolerated, and there is a high possibility that people are not going to tolerate such a person. It has become important to seriously assess whether social change has been better affected by those who rejected God and religion as instruments of oppression or by those who did not negate the importance of God and religion in social life. How long can social activists negate God and religion, which meet the psychological needs of common people? Gandhi's stance was that "As long as you do not teach a lame man to walk, you have no right to remove his crutches." Many people who set out to retire the Gods have reached the age of superannuation, but Gods are far from retirement. One feels that Gandhi had reached a practical assessment that it would be futile to waste his time trying to remove God from homes and society; instead, it would make far better sense to occupy the space offered by God and religion and use it for social betterment. Of course, Gandhi's assessment is always open for debate.

It is important to note that as long as Ram remained with Gandhi, there were no communal riots in the name of Ram. We have experienced how the name of 'Ram' became associated with violence when invoked by those 'committed' to the Ram Mandir – Babri Masjid issue. What is true of Ram is true of the cow as well! As long as the cow was tied in

Gandhi's shed, it remained a gentle creature. The moment the cow was tied in the shed of the Hindutvawadis, it became a violent, wrathful animal. Gandhi's religious stance confused many progressive activists, but the extremist elements did not harbour any such confusion and immediately identified him as their foremost adversary. They realised that, like the proverbial bull in the China shop, Gandhi had destroyed their monopoly over religion. What else could they do but remove Gandhi once and for all?

Today, the entire space of religion is almost occupied by fundamentalist, conservative elements. It is frightening how many so-called Sants, Maharajs, and Buvas. Babas, Yogis, Sadhus, and Sadhvis have used religion to enter politics. 'Gandhi' alone can stop them, but for that, we have to understand Gandhi first.

It is not as if I did not believe in Ram in the past, but my Ram was limited to the one who killed Shambhuk and the one who exiled Sita to the forest. But in the villages, I saw people greet each other with 'Ram Ram', and I, too, ended up returning the greeting with a 'Ram Ram.' Ram, I realised, resided in the hearts of the villagers – this Ram was not the slayer of Shambhuk and the one who exiled Sita; he was someone quite different from the villagers. And this is the Ram whom Gandhi recognised and embraced. Gandhi rejected the story of Ram killing a dalit to study the Vedas as apocryphal and said, "I worship Ram whom I imagine as a *purnapurush*."

Gandhi's conceptualisation of God and Ram created many problems for the leftist activists and even more problems for the extremist sections of the right-wing. If Gandhi had not held on to the space of religion, it would have been even easier to declare him pro-Muslim and denigrate him publicly as such by those who labelled him as Maulana Gandhi and Mohammad Gandhi. Because Gandhi held on to Ram steadfastly and publicly claimed to be a Sanatani Hindu and because he insisted that he loved the Hindu

Dharma with all his being, it hindered the Hindutvawadis' project of denigrating him. In the end, Gandhi did not allow them to reign supreme as the final interpreters of Hindu Dharma.

Hindutvawadis harboured great anger against Gandhi while he lived, and their anger continues even today after he is dead. If this were not so, they would not have been troubled by the fact that after Nathuram shot him, Gandhi's last words were 'Hey Ram' or, according to Pyarelal, 'Ram Ram.' In the play titled 'Mi Nathuram Boltoy', the playwright Pradip Dalvi writes the lines for the character of Nathuram, "As he fell, he uttered only 'uh'!" The Nathuram in this play said, "How could a man who never made any difference between Ram and Rahim, between Krishna and Karim as long as he lived, utter only the name of Ram while dying? Would he not have taken the names of both Ram and Rahim? If at all he wanted to take one name, it would have been Rahim's. After all, Ram resided in his heart and Rahim in his mouth!" There is no evidence that Nathuram actually said these sentences, but by putting the words in the mouth of the character, the extreme right-wing exposed their own anxieties and insecurities. If we understand that Gandhi's Ram caused immense discomfort in the extreme right-wing, then it would surely lead to a lessening of the discomfort of the leftist elements towards Gandhi. It is imperative for the progressive movements in the country today to understand the complexities associated with Gandhi and Ram.

It was important for the extremist right-wing to assert that Gandhi never uttered the name of Ram while dying – they required this to portray Gandhi as pro-Muslim and also to show that he was no 'Mahatma.' Just one day before his death, Gandhi said to Manu, his grand-niece, "If someone fires bullets at me and I die without a groan and with God's name on my lips, then you should tell the world that here was a real Mahatma..." Gandhi received the death that he had prophesied for himself and even in that very last moment of his life, he prevailed over his sworn enemies.

Gandhi entered the social and political scenario in the guise of fighting for independence, but he did not limit himself to political independence. To begin with, he belonged to a caste that was not at the top of India's hierarchical social system or caste system. He belied the prediction that he had emerged out of nowhere as a comet, and soon he would disappear as a comet. If it were only about accepting Gandhi as an exception or for lack of an alternative or out of sheer helplessness, the extremist right-wing would have done that without batting an eyelid, but the problem was that Gandhi was hell-bent on bringing people who lived on the periphery of society into the centre of the freedom struggle. Throughout his life, he tried to bring the untouchables into the centre of public life. He tried to bring women of all castes and sections into the centre of the freedom struggle. The fact remains that women have always been considered unequal by the extremist right-wing who would rather follow the 'laws' of Manu by which women have the sole right to be oppressed. From the perspective of such people, Gandhi had committed a grave sin by talking about the rights of women. Overall, Gandhi's actions were aimed at equalising sections of Indian society, which was not acceptable to the Brahminical supremacists. The only way of stopping Gandhi was for people like Nathuram to physically eliminate him.

Let us look at the range of causes that Gandhi supported and ask whose vested interests were challenged through his activism for such causes – bread labour, farmers' rights, fair wages for workers, public control over temples and democratisation of temple trusts, the demand that the property of temples be used for education, equal rights for the untouchables, putting villages at the centre of public life rather than cities and decentralisation of power, total negation of supremacy based on birth and caste. The fact that he used 'Ram Naam' to bring pressure on temple properties was a cause for much concern among the right-wing. Unfortunately, those who called themselves 'revolutionaries' did not recognise the audacity with which Gandhi set about the task of challenging the status quo and the importance of all-encompassing non-violent actions for the welfare of all classes of people.

It is essential to underline that Gandhi was a Hindu but not a 'Hindutvawadi.' Today, we are facing the terrible outcomes of not making the distinction between Hindu and 'Hindutvawadi' and painting all Hindus with the same brush. The saints of India had recognised the common people's psychological need for faith and religion. Perhaps Dr Babasaheb Ambedkar did not personally require religion, but he recognised this need among his followers, and therefore, he conducted the mass conversion of untouchables to Buddhism. Many revolutionary activists made the useless argument that this conversion was not about Hindu Dharma but about Buddhist Dhamma – and in doing so, they completely side-lined the main issue about the importance of faith in human existence. Marxists who negate religion, calling it the opium of the masses, ruled West Bengal for several decades and yet the masses of Bengal did not lose the attraction for Durga Puja. There was a time when the communists were powerful leaders of the trade union movement in Mumbai, and yet the workers did not lose interest in celebrating Ganeshotsav.

Gandhi was astute enough to understand that since the masses needed deities and religion, and therefore he held on steadfastly to religion. We have to understand Gandhi in the modern context, and for that, we have to distinguish between Hindu and Hindutvawadi. Gandhi had made this distinction. In fact, the extremist right-wing Hindutvawadi should not be considered Hindus at all. In order to understand the difference between Hindu and Hindutvawadi, we can take the example of the cow and the tick. The tick sits on the back of the cow, and the blood of the cow is inside the tick, but that does not mean the tick becomes a cow by sucking its blood! The extremist sections of Hindutvawadis are like ticks on the body of the 'Hindu' - if at all there is a relationship between Hindu and Hindutvawadi, it can be described as that between the oppressor and the oppressed. Hindutvawadi is the oppressor, and the Hindu is the oppressed.

Those who attack Hindus with the aim of attacking Hindutvawadis make the mistake of beating the cow with the aim of getting rid of the tick on its back. The tick does not die; it does not even fall off the back, but the cow is injured in the beating. And therefore, the cow that should have been with social activists is today helplessly standing before the butcher who holds a knife to her neck.

Dr Bhupendranath Datta, the brother of Swami Vivekananda, has written a detailed biography of Swamiji titled 'Swami Prophet – Patriot Prophet' in which he writes that Vivekananda used religion and spirituality as innovative instruments for socialist transformation. Swami Vivekananda would say in jest that if anybody stepped out of his home in saffron, he could be sure that people would give him at least one meal a day. Things have changed since then – today, people wearing saffron are often suspected as tricksters and opportunists out to grab political power under the garb of being sadhus. However, this only goes to show that the saffron continues to wield power and represents religion and spirituality in the minds of the common people. Swami Vivekananda used the power of saffron to feed the poor; today, people are using it to gain personal wealth.

Swami Vivekananda donned the saffron garb to harness the power of saffron for the greater good. Gandhi, too, used the power of religion for the common good. Unfortunately, the so-called progressive activists did not accord either of them the place they deserved in the centre of the socio-political movement. Such progressive movements shunned Swami Vivekananda and left him at the mercy of the Hindutvawadis, who gleefully destroyed his reformist-revolutionary agenda. They buried his reformist-revolutionary agenda beneath the massive memorials they constructed in his name. Gandhi is on the verge of suffering the same fate.

Swami Vivekananda once said, "Learning and wisdom are superfluities; the surface glitters merely, but the heart is the seat of all power. It is not in the brain but in the heart that the Atman, possessed of knowledge, power, and activity, has its seat." While we may not fully agree with Swami Vivekananda, yet we must consider how terrible it would be if the language of the heart does not find any place in the vocabulary of revolution. If compassion is removed from revolution, all that would remain is cruelty. Many revolutionaries point out with great pride that although Sant Gadge Maharaj went to Pandharpur, he never stepped inside the temple of Lord Vitthal. And yet, the same Gandge Maharaj constructed Dharamshala for the pilgrims who came from faraway places to Pandharpur. Gadge Maharaj's Dharamshala in Pandharpur is an expression of the heart. It is the same soulful expression that we find in his bhajan: 'Gopala Gopala devakinandan Gopala.' It is the same expression that imbues Sant Tukarm's 'Vithal Vithal.' Gandhi's soul, too, finds expression in *Raghupati raghav raja ram.'* It is the soul alone that can communicate with another soul. Gandhi knew the power of religion and religious expressions.

Throughout his life, he tried to harness this power to bring positive changes to the lives of the people.

It is important to understand Gandhi's actions as much as his words. We make a grave mistake if we do not look at the actions behind Gandhi's words, especially when he said, "I am a Sanatani Hindu." We have to consider that there is a self-confessed Sanatani Hindu who never entered a temple and did not spend time on traditional forms of worship, rites and rituals. He does not have a deity in his house, not even a photograph. Therefore, the questions of daily worship, incense burning, and offerings do not arise. What kind of a Sanatani is this? "I believe in the Varna system," said Gandhi and yet he blissfully and quite inexplicably supports the mixing of occupations and inter-marrying of castes. Gandhi is the only man in the world who is extremely religious and at the same time completely secular at the same time. He is undoubtedly a difficult code to crack.

Gandhi is constantly attacked for being pro-Muslim and for following a policy of Muslim appeasement. This accusation does not make sense in light of the Muslim League's declaration of Gandhi as their enemy. How is this possible? How can the same person be pro-Muslim as far as the Hindu right-wing is concerned and pro-Hindu as far as the Muslim League is concerned? How can one analyse this situation? When Gandhi rushes to stop the communal riots in Noakhali, he is decried by the Muslim League as pro-Hindu, and when the same Gandhi rushes to stop the communal riots in Bihar, he is labelled pro-Muslim by the Hindutvawadis. On the one hand, Gandhi was accused of insulting Jinnah, which led the latter to demand Pakistan, and yet, on the other hand, Gandhi was also accused of unnecessarily pampering Jinnah's demands for Pakistan.

There is a question that haunts us – why did Gandhi appease Muslims if at all he did so? It is quite understandable when politicians today are accused of appeasing Muslims because they want to make some electoral gains out of it by getting Muslim votes. Without such votes, there is the fear of losing the election, and if they lose their seat, they will lose political power. But Gandhi certainly did not aim to increase his vote tally. He was not after winning an election. If he had been after political power, then he would have been in Delhi on the day India won independence. The fact remains that the very man who had led the country to victory was absent from the celebrations. He was far away in Noakhali, trying to provide relief to riot-torn communities.

Although Gandhi did not fight for political power, he certainly did fight for gaining independence from foreign rule, and it was important for him that Hindus and Muslims should come together in the struggle for freedom. He knew that without unity, there was no strength, and without strength, the country could never achieve independence. The problem of Hindu-Muslim unity was not a new one. It was already a problem even before Gandhi came into the picture. In fact, both factions of Congress

– moderates as well as extremists – did try for communal unity. The British policy of 'divide-and-rule' was, of course, opposed to such unity. Whether it was Justice Ranade or Gopal Krishna Gokhale, all leaders were in favour of Hindu – Muslim unity. Even Lokmanya Tilak was gravely aware of the importance of communal unity. The leaders were also aware of the propensity of the British to create obstructions to such unity by favouring the Muslims. Therefore, many of them were of the opinion that it would serve the cause of unity if they agreed to a more favourable deal for the Muslims. Even Swami Vivekananda was of the opinion that Muslim interests should be protected at all costs. The point to note is that none of the other leaders were labelled 'pro-Muslim' – such a label was reserved for Gandhi alone.

In a lecture Swami Vivekananda delivered on "The Future of India", he said, "Even to the Mohammedan Rule, we owe that great blessing, the destruction of exclusive privilege. That rule was, after all, not all bad; nothing is all bad, and nothing is all good. The Mohammedan conquest of India came as a salvation to the downtrodden and to the poor. That is why one-fifth of our people have become Mohammedans. It was not the sword that did it all. It would be the height of madness to think it was all the work of sword and fire." It is extremely puzzling that such assertions by Swami Vivekananda did not draw the wrath of the Hindutvavadis. In his speech delivered in California on 25 March 1900, Swami Vivekananda said that the unique quality of Islam that sets it apart is the simplicity of its tenets. There is no multiplicity of principles and interpretations in this religion. The second quality is its emphasis on equality - all human beings are equal before god, and there is no priest or middleman between god and humans. Can it be said that Swami Vivekananda was praising Islam to appease Muslims? At least the Hindutvavadis did not say so! On the contrary, they are more interested in trapping Swami Vivekananda in magnificently constructed memorials without paying much attention to his philosophy or tenets.

Much before the advent of Gandhi, Justice Mahadev Govind Ranade promoted Hindu-Muslim unity. He said, "In this vast country, no progress is possible unless both Hindus and Mahomedans join hands together and are determined to follow the lead of men who flourished in Akbar's time."

Lokmanya Tilak signed the famous Lucknow Pact to bring together the two communities for 'swarajya.' Under this Pact, Muslims were granted separate electorates, which sowed the seeds of partition. And yet, no one condemned Tilak as being pro-Muslim, and no one accused him of Muslim appeasement. In fact, Tilak's vision at the time was that a liberal attitude towards Muslim representation was needed for unity between the two countries. Speaking on the Lucknow Pact, he said it would convert the triangular fight between Hindus, Muslims and the British into a two-way fight between Hindus and Muslims fighting together on one side and the British on the other. Tilak called the Lucknow Pact 'The Luck Now Pact.'

Tilak said in his speech, "It has been said that we, Hindus, have yielded too much. The concession that has been made to our Muhammadan brethren in the Legislative Council is really nothing too much. In proportion to the concession that had been made to the Muslims, their enthusiasm and warm-hearted support is surely greater. I urge the audience to actively give effect to the resolution adopted by Congress."

Tilak was aware that without the support of the Muslims and without both Hindus and Muslims working together, freedom was an impossible dream. He had experienced how the British would offer concessions to Muslims in order to splinter them from the freedom struggle. In one speech, Tilak compared the British and Muslim rules in India by saying that although both were foreign invaders, the Muslim rulers came to consider this country as their own, and they did not remove wealth from this country to other lands. The British drained the wealth of this country in order to enrich Britain. The question is, was Tilak trying to appease Muslims when he came to this conclusion?

In 1905, while opposing the partition of Bengal, Tilak went to the extent of saying that in future, a Shivaji may rise from amongst the Muslims. In spite of making such a blatantly pro-Muslim statement, the Hindutvawadis did not attack him for this stance. They did not call him Mohammad Tilak or Maulana Tilak as they did with Gandhi.

The challenge of Hindu-Muslim unity that Tilak faced was also faced by Gandhi. He was tasked with leading forward the freedom struggle against the British colonial rule. The British continued with the divide-and-rule policy as before. The baton of leadership had passed from Tilak to Gandhi. However, with the transfer of leadership came a shift in the understanding of why India wanted freedom and who should benefit from independence. Gandhi interrogated the long-term vision of swaraj at the centre of the struggle. Would it be freedom for the elites or for the masses? Would it benefit the slothful elites or those who live by the dint of their labour? Would it benefit the upper castes, upper classes or the poorest of the poor? Who would get the franchise – the well-to-do, the well-educated or each person who belonged to the country?

Gandhi brought these queries along with him, even as he entered the national struggle. Not only this, he made it his life's mission to include those who remained at the periphery of national life as equal participants in the struggle. Farmers, labourers, workers, untouchables, and women were brought into the mainstream of the struggle and, thereby, into the mainstream of public life. Obviously, the upper caste elites who considered themselves the rightful inheritors of political power were disturbed by Gandhi's actions. The powerful sections who enjoyed their privileges by birth felt threatened. Therefore, it became impertinent for them to assert that 'freedom' means 'political freedom'; it does not mean 'social freedom' or 'social equality' and based on that assertion, they had opposed Gandhi tooth and nail. This opposition consisted of accusations and falsehoods spread against Gandhi. When such false propaganda and hate speeches did not hurt Gandhi's popularity or leadership, they were 'forced' to assassinate him.

Those who hate Gandhi continue to spread hatred against him even after his death. And yet there continued to be people like Pandit Kumar Gandharva who dedicated a *Raag* to Gandhi called Gandhi Malhar. Standing in the centre of intense hatred on one side and intense love on the other, Gandhi continues to smile mischievously. He stood his ground yesterday as he does today and will continue to do so in the future.

★ ★ ★

CHAPTER 8

CONFUSION LEADS TO ASSASSINATION

It appears that one section of the right-wing has more or less succeeded in its nefarious agenda of representing Gandhi as a Muslim lover and, therefore, quite naturally responsible for the creation of Pakistan. They argue that in such a situation, patriots and nationalists such as Nathuram Godse and his equally nationalist companions had little choice but to assassinate Gandhi, which was also an act of nationalism. They represent Gandhi as a sinner, someone who favoured Pakistan more than his own country and Nathuram as a saint because he favoured Bharat Mata. Gandhi is anti-national because he loves Pakistan more than Bharat Mata, and Nathuram was a patriot because out of his extreme patriotism, he killed the anti-national Gandhi. Moreover, the murder of a sinner should not be called murder at all. To begin with, the word in Marathi for murder, 'khoon', entered the Marathi language from the language of the 'Muslim invaders', therefore the defenders of culture should avoid using such words in the first place and opt for either 'hatya' or 'wash.' Of these two, *Katya* is used for the good people, a category to which Gandhi did not belong; thus, according to their logic, *it* is the proper word for Gandhi, the sinner. This is the etymology of the Marathi word *gandhiwadh* or extermination of Gandhi. The word *wadh* is usually reserved for mythological antagonistic figures like Ravan, Kansa, Shishupala, Jayadrath, Jarasandh, Duryodhan and Dushasan. The invader Afzal Khan, who laid siege on *swaraj*, was killed by Chhatrapati Shivaji and his intestines were pulled out – that was *wadh*. Gandhi, according to his opponents, deserves the word *wadh*. *Wadh* encompasses the meanings of other descriptors like demon, evil, wicked, and sinner – there is no need to use these other words because these are the very people who are required to be slayed, whose *wadh* needs to be committed.

No adjectives are required for Nathuram because once it is established that the one who is slain is the demon, evil, wicked, or sinner, it automatically makes Nathuram god-like, righteous, noble and saintly. We had only heard of the idiom 'killing two birds with one stone', but the single word '*gandhiwadh*' used by Hindutvawadis has killed more birds than one can count.

When the trial of Gandhi's assassination started, it was reported in certain newspapers as 'charges of *gandhiwadh*.' Well, not every trial is reported as a trial of '*wadh*.' It is described in reports as the murder trial of such and such. Pradeep Dalvi, in the play '*Mi Nathuram Boltoy*', uses the word '*gandhiwadh*.' Now, Pradeep Dalvi, the playwright, does not use the word '*wadh*' in every script that he writes. There was a play in Pune on the Joshi-Abhayankar murder by Jakkal Sutar. In that play, the word used was 'murder of Joshi-Abhyankar', not their *wadh*. Actually, according to the traditionalist Brahminical worldview, there cannot be a *wadh* of a Brahmin no matter how wicked, lascivious or evil he may be – there can only be a heinous murder, a terrible '*brahmhatya*.' If Pradeep Dalvi had written on the trial of the murder of Joshi-Abhaynkar, he would have named it the 'Joshi-Abhyankar Brahmhatya trial', which would have been considered quite appropriate by his compatriots.

Let me say that in the very first scene of Dalvi's play, Tatyarao said, "Are you mad? I did not wish you a long life. I wished you immortal life … you have become immortal Nathuram. The moment you pressed the trigger of the pistol and Gandhi died, that very moment you became immortal. It would be a matter of debate whether you ended Gandhism, but you have slayed Gandhi and you have survived." Indeed for Hindutvawadis, Nathuram's act killed Gandhi and Nathuram survived, beyond that Nathuram becomes immortal. Why? Because he kills an evil man named Gandhi.

It is the misfortune of Nathuramwadis that they have committed a saintly act by slaying the wicked, evil sinner demon called Gandhi but have to defend themselves by invoking the same 'sinner' called Gandhi. Their hatred, envy and malice toward Gandhi went to such extremes that after the murder, they celebrated the heinous act in different places, distributed sweets, and when the tables were turned on them, they pulled him close and made him part of their *pratahsmaraniya* morning prayers. It is claimed that although Nathuram killed Gandhi, he had great love for Gandhi and bent down to touch his feet before shooting him at point-blank range.

Once, a Nathuram-lover tried to confuse me by describing Nathuram's qualities. "Nathuram was a learned person, well-educated, highly erudite. Would he kill somebody without any reason?" he argued.

I said, "Am I educated?"

"Yes," he answered.

"Am I well-read, thoughtful? Are you aware that I was an editor?"

Once again, he said with great respect, "Yes."

"Suppose I go near a woman and wish her politely with a namaskar, then I touch her feet to pay respect, and then I rape and kill her. Would you say that I had a lot of respect for her? Would you defend my act by pointing out that I am an educated person, a thinker, writer and former editor?"

My questions threw him into confusion. It was obvious that by highlighting Nathuram's sense of fair play and education, he sought to defend the dastardly act of Gandhi's assassin.

In the play 'Mi Nathuram Boltoy', the murderer is provided with enough scope to rant against Gandhi. Any opposition to the rant is immediately answered by invoking the right to freedom of speech and expression. It is ironic that the people who are ready to support Nathuram's rights remain silent about the fact that Nathuram not only took away Gandhi's right to speak but even his right to life. Nathuram is free to use the term *wadh* for the cold-blooded murder, and Gopal Godse is allowed to use the term *hatya* in his memoir's title, 'Gandhi Hatya ani Mi.' No matter what the Hindutvavadis assert, Nathuram was never a Gandhi-bhakt. He did not have the slightest respect for Gandhi.

"I will live 125 years", said Gandhi, and it is as if Nathuram retorted arrogantly, "But who will allow you to live?" And yet, while creating 'Mi Nathuram Boltoy, ' the character is made to utter words like, "…of course he was great. There is no need for me to either accept or deny the truth. His courageous fight against racism is admirable. It is admirable how he went around the countryside to understand India after returning to India. It was courageous of him to announce from the platform of Congress that lawyers from Delhi and Mumbai, like Nehru-Jinnah-Patel, cannot represent India. Salt satyagrha, Dandi

Yatra, the Quit India Movement, and the burning of foreign cloth – I became his supporter because of all these acts. When Gandhi was arrested at that time, *'sabarmati sant jail ma chhe'* was the slogan on my lips.' All these words are utter falsehoods put in the mouth of Nathuram – a veritable bazaar of hypocrisy and duplicity. The murderers of Gandhi never had any love for him, but they recognised the people's love for him, and therefore, their hatred and malice are first wrapped in false claims of love. After establishing Nathuram's 'love' for Gandhi, the bogey of 'Muslim love' is raised through the false allegations of Gandhi gifting away Rs.55 crores to Pakistan and fasting for it.

Let us examine the truth behind this allegation. When the country was partitioned, the situation was like the division of family wealth between two brothers. Prior to the partition, the assets and liabilities were divided to the tune of Rs.375 crores in the Reserve Bank of India. Of this, Rs. 75 crores was earmarked for Pakistan and the rest for India. Rs. 20 crore was handed over to Pakistan immediately, and the balance of Rs.55 crore was to be handed over at a later date. This treaty was signed under Lord Mountbatten. Representatives of both countries were present. Liaqat Ali and Ghulam Mohammed represented Pakistan, while Nehru and Patel represented India. Mountbatten read out a memorandum before the Prime Ministers of both countries according to which the condition of giving Rs. 55 crores to Pakistan would not be considered final till all issues pertaining to partition were settled. This was an international agreement between two countries. Rs.20 crores had been handed over to Pakistan out of its share of Rs. 75 crores. Rs.55 crores remained to be handed over. This agreement had nothing to do with Gandhi. The negotiations were conducted by Nehru and Patel, and they agreed upon them.

'Sow confusion amidst all' is a favourite strategy followed by the extremists. Accordingly, they converted the rightful share of Pakistan under the agreement into a donation, charity or subsidy. Naturally, by referring to the share as a donation or subsidy, they sought to change the context entirely.

It was a time when Pakistan was considered an enemy nation by a large section of the public, and that, too, was a Muslim nation carved out of India after bloody Hindu-Muslim riots during partition. Blood flowed on the streets, corpses piled up – corpses of both Hindus and Muslims. In such a poisonous atmosphere, if anyone said that Mahatma Gandhi has announced, 'give Rs.55 crores to Pakistan' and further, if they don't inform that the amount is owed to Pakistan under a bilateral agreement, then what sort of impact would it create? They go on to say that Gandhi fasted on 13 January 1948 with the intention of pouring not oil but petrol into the fiery situation.

Converting the amount owed under the agreement into a donation or subsidy helps Hindutvavadis paint Gandhi as a Muslim lover and a Pakistan supporter. The truth is that Gandhi did not fast for this issue at all, but Hindutvavadis conveniently used this as a pretext to assassinate Gandhi. Who, according to them, is responsible for the partition of India? – Gandhi. Gandhi is not a nationalist at all, and therefore, he does not have the right to remain alive, and an avatar like Nathuram descends upon the earth to 'slay' Gandhi.

It is to be considered that India had just emerged as a new and independent nation in the world. At such a time, if India had not upheld a bilateral agreement, it would have destroyed India's reputation in the international community. It would have been marked as an unreliable nation that did not live up to its commitments. How proper would it have been for a new country to earn such a stigma? How is it that Gandhi, who worked to prevent such a stigma, is considered an anti-national and those who spread half-truths to provoke people are patriots? Those who did not fight for the freedom of this country cannot suddenly claim that they are hypersensitive about the honour of the nation. And yet, how is Nathuram a patriot?

And at the end of it all, isn't there something called morality? A word, once given, should be fulfilled; it should not be discarded. On the one hand they sing the praise of traditions, sing the praise of 'raghukul reet sada chali ayi, prran jaye par vachan na jayi' and on the other hand when Gandhi insisted on following up on a promise, they mark him a traitor?

The reasons and explanations given by assassins and their supporters for Gandhi's assassination on 30 January 1948 are that he was pro-Muslim, Pakistan lover and that he insisted on giving Rs.55 Crores to Pakistan. These are, of course, the motives narrated by Nathuram in his nine-hour-long speech in the court during his trial. This narrative gives rise to the counter-question about the attempt on Gandhi's life made in 1934 at Pune. These same fundamentalist elements were involved in that assassination attempt as well. What were the reasons at that time? Even the word 'Pakistan' was yet to be born at that time, and 'partition' had not even been imagined. There was no question of 'partition', and because 'partition' had not taken place, there was no question of handing over Rs.55 crores. So why was there an attack on Gandhi?

Suppose the attempt in 1934 had been successful. What reasons would have been put forward as justification? At that time, Gandhi's long and intense Harijan Yatra was going on. They could certainly not have confessed that we slayed Gandhi because he was doing the work of Harijan upliftment. They would have also found it difficult to say that they had slayed Gandhi because he wanted to bring the *bhangi*, the barber and the lawyer on the same social level. Gandhi had issued a massive challenge to the traditional argument that since the Brahmins had lost their power to the British, the Brahmins had the right to reclaim power and wield it at pleasure. And yet, they would never have been able to say that they killed Gandhi because he shattered their dreams. So what reasons would these people have presented? This is a question that disturbs us to this day.

Gandhi's first biography in Marathi was written by Avantikabai Gokhale, and Lokmanya Tilak penned the foreword. In it, he said, "The importance that I placed on piety in character, looking from that perspective, the character of Mahatma Gandhi is certainly one that should be considered ideal by ordinary people." Tilak said this, and yet, except for a few honourable exceptions, the supporters of Tilak harbour a lifelong hatred for Gandhi.

On 26 December 1934, the Sarsanghachalak Dr. Hegdewar met Gandhi and sought his blessings. He said, "If your wishes are with us, then we shall certainly be successful in our efforts." Which success was he talking about when Dr. Hegdewar uttered these words? Dr. Shyamaprasad Mukherjee writes that after the death of Gandhi, his demise was a lightning shock for the nation. "When the entire world was trying to find a way through darkness, Gandhi showed the way. Today, the light has died out. His death is the greatest assault on this nation. He was everyone's friend; he did not have enemies…." Shyamaprasad's followers act in direct opposition to the sentiments he expresses. Golwalkar Guruji wrote an article on the occasion of Gandhi's centenary on 2 October 1969 in a Marathi monthly magazine called *Yugvani* published from Nagpur. He writes, "Not only are his thoughts and his innumerable great qualities ignored, but the heart is filled with sorrow to see the manner in which he is caricatured." Upon reading these lines, one wonders who he is referring to.

If Gandhi had died in the assassination attempt of 1934 at Pune, what excuse would they have placed before the world? This question disturbs me as much as the statements of the renowned men mentioned above. One almost wonders whether it was Nathuram and his gang who assassinated Gandhi or whether Gandhi picked up the pistol to shoot himself, thereby committing suicide and somehow managing to frame Nathuram. This thought disturbs me as well. And then I wonder whether the statements of these respected men are nothing but yet another attempt at sowing seeds of confusion.

★ ★ ★

CHAPTER 9

A FISTFUL OF FIERY SALT

D.N. Gokhale has written the book *Gandhi: Manav ki Mahamanv* on the life of Gandhi. In his introduction, he states that the book should be read as a biography, not an analysis of Gandhi's personality. The author is a follower of the Hindutvawadi line of thought and influenced by the RSS. Perhaps he came across Gandhi while working under Sawarkar. He writes, "I sat in the vehicle of Savarkar's Hindutva and reached Gandhigram." It seems that he was requested to write the biographies of Dr. Hedgewar or Golwalkar Guruji, but his choice fell on Gandhi. "Both of them are my ideals, but I did not undertake to write their biographies because there was nothing to attract me from the literary perspective. But I felt like writing about Gandhi because Gandhi's character has powerful events that can change the course of entire nations - there are ups and downs, pace, excitement and drama. There is saintly virtue and deep enigmatic traits. There is a profound struggle against circumstances, against social structures and internal dispositions. It is a light that travels far through darkness, storms, and solitude. Many things attracted me, and I decided to study Gandhi's biography. In particular, I liked the mysteries in Gandhi's character, which throw a challenge to analyses along with the dazzling purity and humanity which thrills us, and my decision became final."

Authors around the world were attracted to Gandhi, and perhaps they wrote for the same reasons that D.N. Gokhale expressed. A huge and growing corpus of world literature has been created around Gandhi. The number of dramas and cinemas in Gandhi is substantial as well. If we look at the single event of Salt Satyagraha in Gandhi's life, we recognise the dramatic aspects which D. N Gokhale mentions.

Gandhi started out to walk 200 miles from Sabarmati to Dandi with a handful of people (seventy-eight to be exact) to pick up a pinch of salt. Why? Because it was said that the sun never set in the British empire, and Gandhi wanted the sun to set. Honestly speaking, his actions appear to be comic. A mouse challenges a huge elephant. People must have bared their teeth and laughed. People were right to laugh. Opponents made fun of him, and Gandhi's own followers were upset by such comical acts.

Those who propounded the philosophy of freedom through bloodshed found a fresh opportunity against him. Gandhi is now performing the Salt Satyagraha; next, it will be a turmeric Satyagraha and, thereafter, a chilly Satyagraha. Does anyone ever get independence by performing Satyagraha of salt, turmeric and chillies?

Even Gandhi's colleagues did not like the idea of Salt Satyagraha. Jawaharlal Nehru was quite upset. Motilal Nehru wrote a long letter scolding Gandhi about this decision. Vallabhbhai Patel was so angry that he boycotted the meeting that Gandhi called for planning the Salt Satyagraha. Indulal Yagnik derided the decision, saying that this was a case of 'killing the fly of salt laws with the hammer of Satyagraha.'

In the British corridors and with the supporters of the Raj, the matter was one of jest. "Let Gandhi eat his own salt quickly," was the opinion. The British-owned newspaper published from Kolkata called *The Statesman* commented, "…it is difficult not to laugh, and that must be the mood of most thinking Indians." According to the editorial, it was childish drama on the part of Gandhi to challenge the sovereignty of the government over salt in this manner.

No matter what his own people or others said about the Salt Satyagraha, Gandhi could see the volcano hidden in its womb. This is why he said, "Either I shall return with what I want, or my dead body will float in the ocean." He would say that if they died, they would go to heaven; if they were arrested, they would go to prison; and if they were victorious, they would return home.

Even when others did not realise the intensity of the Satyagraha, Gandhi was fully aware of it, and therefore, he predicted the future of death or imprisonment. Movements have their own science and skills. It requires a proper understanding of the situation and a finger on the pulse of the people, providing space for people's participation, making it easy and simple to understand, and, most importantly, the issue should touch the hearts of ordinary people. Salt is directly related to each person. The very taste of food is in salt. A person may be poor or rich, a woman or man or belonging to whichever caste, religion, language or region; this is an issue that everyone understands immediately. The issue in Champaran was related to farmers, as well as the farmers who produced indigo. Kheda and bardoli issues were also limited to farmers. In Ahmedabad, the issue was limited to labourers and textile workers. Although these movements were limited in their scope, they did contribute to the larger awakening in society. However, wide-ranging participation was not possible in these movements. But salt was an entirely different matter. Gandhi, the skilled commander, definitely foresaw that ordinary people would be able to participate directly in large numbers. The Salt Satyagraha was announced, and there was a country-wide response to the announcement.

The same Vallabhbhai Patel, who thought that the movement did not have any strength at all, was arrested by the British. Even more, the movement started, thereby making evident the strength of the Satyagraha. Motilal

Nehru had written a long letter against the useless movement, to which Gandhi replied in two words, '*Karke dekho* – act and see,' on a postcard. Later, the British government arrested Motilal Nehru and imprisoned him. Motilal Nehru sent a postcard to Gandhi from prison with two words, '*karke dekha* – acted and saw.'

The moment Gandhi announced the programme, a debate ensued among the British on whether to immediately arrest Gandhi. If he was immediately arrested, it would unnecessarily increase his importance, and his arrest would invoke reactions. Therefore, instead of arresting him on the spot, it was decided to wait till the movement had run steam, at which point the British could step in and arrest him on charges of breaking the law.

The Dandi March started on 12 March 1930. It would take around 24 days to walk 200 miles. This 61-year-old man left home with his handful of companions to pick a pinch of salt. Sixty years is considered the age of retirement, but even at that age, the man was walking 12 miles in a day. He could have travelled by motor, but how could he have connected with the villages on the way, with the common people? How could direct contact between hearts be made possible? Didn't the skillful commander already know this? There were horses kept ready in case he found it difficult to walk. But this clever man needed neither camels nor horses.

The man's calculations were straightforward and accurate. Before the Dandi Yatra started, he said in the prayer evening meeting at the ashram, "Suppose ten men in each of the seven lacs of villages in India come forward to manufacture salt and disobey the Salt Act; what do you think this government can do? Even the worst autocrat would not dare to blow regiments of peaceful resisters out of a cannon's mouth."

The wildfire of Satyagraha started to spread. There were more than two thousand people in the evening prayer before the Dandi March started.

The commander had prepared minutely for the non-violent war before the war started - if the commander was arrested, then who would take over, and suppose even he was arrested then would take over the reins thereafter, who would lead the different sections, how should the one behave when faced with arrest. Codes of conduct were drawn up for the seventy-eight soldiers. What should be done at the soldier camp? What type of information was to be collected at the village where they halted for the night? The demographics of the village (the population of women, men, Hindus, Muslims, Christians, Parsis, etc.), number of untouchables and the situation of those who were undergoing education, the number of girls and boys enrolled in the village school if any, number of situation of livestock, number of people who spin charkha and use khadi, total amounts collected as land revenue and rate thereof, the extent of public grazing lands and finally the amount of salt consumed. All this information was gathered as part of the training of soldiers and increased in the commander's database.

Even in the midst of this struggle, Gandhiji never lost his focus on social issues. In one village, Gandhi crossed the village temple and square and walked straight to the shanties of the untouchables. There, he fetched water from the well with his own hand and bathed at the well. On seeing this, the upper caste people of the village said, "If he wanted to purify himself by bathing, he should have used 'pure' water instead of the 'impure' water of the untouchables. And if at all he wanted water from that well, he should have asked a servant to fetch it."

In one village, Gandhi asked that the untouchables should be allowed to attend the public meeting. How could they refuse his request? However, several upper caste women left the meeting after the untouchables came to sit there. Even while fighting a political war, Gandhi remained aware of the struggle for social freedom. Those who argued that political freedom took precedence over social freedom discredited social freedom. They blamed Gandhi for discrediting the freedom struggle by including social issues in its ambit, and therefore, quite naturally, they remained aloof from this 'impure' freedom struggle. It was logical for them to consider Gandhi to be at the top of their list of enemies and to oppose him, and if he did not bow to that opposition, it was logical for them to kill him. But when the very people for whom Gandhi put his life on the line accuse him by saying 'he was casteist', then it does not appear to be logical at all, not from any perspective whatsoever.

We know of the great penance that Gandhi underwent to align himself in every way with the common man. The world is thrilled by the journey of the barrister Gandhi in suit to the Gandhi in loincloth. Two people out of the trained seventy-eight soldiers in Dandi yatra commit some small mistake, but this strict commander does not cover up their mistakes and instead speaks about it openly in public and also undertakes punishment on their behalf. One out of these seventy-eight gives in to the temptation of eating ice cream during a halt, and the other asks a servant to carry a petromax lamp on his head and walk fast. Gandhi, in his speech during the halt, said, "We may not consider anybody low. I observed that you had provided for the night journey a heavy kerosene burner mounted on a stool which a poor labourer carried on his head. This was a humiliating sight. This man was being goaded to walk fast. I could not bear the sight. I, therefore, put on speed and outraced the whole company. But it was no use. The man was made to run after me. The humiliation was complete. If the weight had to be carried, I should have loved to see someone among ourselves carrying it. We would then soon dispense both with the stool and the burner. No labourer would carry such a load on his head. We rightly object to *begar* (forced labour). But what was this if it was not *begar*? Remember that in swaraj, we would expect one drawn from the so-called lower class to preside over India's destiny." Truth be told, we are so used to leaders saying, 'small incidents are bound to happen in big cities' that we would have accepted Gandhi saying, 'small incidents are bound to happen in such a massive battle.' But Gandhi does not say so. Nobody has taken him to task, and therefore, it was not expected that he would say anything.

He, of his own volition, decides to bring the mistake before the public. These are the seemingly small incidents that set him apart, and he appears to be 'different' from all others. Perhaps it is this difference that earned him the name 'Mahatma.'

Gandhi's caravan walked towards Dandi. Every day, the numbers in that caravan multiply. Villages on the way eagerly welcomed them, and not just the numbers but the news of the caravan multiples spread across the country and filled people with the awakening for independence. It is natural for British officials to assess that they must do something before the energy being created leads to an explosion. There is an uneasy stirring in the officialdom. Should they arrest Gandhi or let him go? He would move ahead if set free, but his arrest might lead to sharp public reactions. Confusion and chaos reign supreme. Further, someone has informed Irwin that Gandhi's blood pressure has reached dangerous levels and the condition of the heart is not too good either. Because of the physical and mental strains, he might die before reaching Dandi. The British government are hopeful that such an eventuality would release them of the pressure without their having to do much.

Dandi Yatra moves ahead. There is great excitement and expectation across the country about what will happen in Dandi. Not just newspapers of the country but also foreign ones reach Dandi to cover the fight for 'justice against injustice.'

On 5 April 1930, Gandhi reaches Dandi. The next morning, Gandhi bathed in the sea, and then he walked to a place where there was salt. He lifted a pinch of salt and showed the salt to the great mass of people who had congregated there. Gandhi had defied the law of the British government by lifting a pinch of salt, and that too openly. Sarojini Naidu immediately addressed him as a 'law-breaker.'

Even there, the *bania* (trader community) inside Gandhi was awake. Such a big movement requires resources. The movement had a stomach, didn't it? And who else but Bapu was concerned about the stomach? The *ardha tola* pinch of salt lifted by Gandhi was auctioned by him and was sold for Rs. 525. At that time, the price of *ardha tola* of pure gold was Rs.40, and this man sold *ardha tola* of impure salt for Rs.525 – yes, the salt was impure because the British police had already removed all the pure salt. It is unfortunate that the man who could fetch the price of gold for garbage was reduced to 'garbage' by his detractors.

The physical body is a reality, and some people build a strong physique through exercise. Similarly, everyone uses words, but there are some who make their words strong through their actions. Words, too, have to be strengthened. When we say, "Their words carry weight", what does it mean? The strength comes when the person using certain words also acts upon them. Whatever weight, price, strength and sharpness, Gandhi's words had come from the manner in which he lived his life. When he asks people to be prepared for death, he himself is equally prepared and waiting. His followers were convinced of this and, therefore, followed him without a shadow of a doubt. Just as an empty sack cannot stand, similarly empty words too cannot stand - they have to be filled with life experiences. The journey of the Barrister Mohandas Karamchand Gandhi in his suit to the Mahatma Gandhi in his loincloth contains the experiences of the man, and that is why his words stood their test, and people believed in him.

The Indian people were told to break the salt laws. Before telling the people to do so, he himself picked up a pinch of salt and broke the law. He first performed the act and then asked others to follow, and then all over the country, people started breaking the salt law like wildfire with the objective of not allowing Gandhi's words to go in vain. The very same Jawaharlal Nehru, who was dissatisfied with this programme, later described the Satyagraha as a 'fire on the prairie.'

In the days following the moment when Gandhi picked up a pinch of salt, people across the country started to follow the act. In hundreds of places, salt was illegally produced and illegally transported, illegally bought and sold. The British government initiated repressive measures on a mass scale. Across the country, those who broke the salt laws were arrested. There were lathi charges and shootouts – news poured in from every corner of the country. The news of the arrest of leaders of the freedom struggles started to pour in. The *khidmatgars* were angered by the arrest of Khan Abdul Gafar Khan, and they protested in Peshawar. They faced the hooves of horses, machine guns and lathi charges. In Peshawar, a police officer ran a motor car into a mass of protestors, killing seventy people. The response to this repression was so massive that for the next five days, Peshawar was ruled not by the British but by the *khudai khidmatgars*, who broke the salt law.

Those who laughed at Gandhi's Salt Satyagraha were forced to eat humble pie. Those who made fun of him had to swallow their words. Even Irwin confessed that he was surprised at the support received by the protest. On top of that, there was no place in the prisons to hold so many Satyagrahis. And how long could they hold such large numbers? The government found a way out. Instead of arresting them, the protestors were beaten up wherever they were caught. The British followed the brutal policy of breaking the bones of those who broke the law. The surprising thing was that while many of the leaders of the movement were arrested and imprisoned, the government had not touched the chief brain behind the protests – Gandhi.

Perhaps the government was hopeful that during this time, Gandhi's blood pressure would increase and his weak heart would fail all of a sudden during this high-tension protest. Either they were hopeful, or perhaps they were sanguine that they would achieve their goal without lifting a finger. Thus, Gandhi was free. He was travelling ceaselessly from one place to another, and the fire was spreading wherever he went. Gandhi announced that at the end of April, he would raid three government salt godowns in Dharasana in Gujarat, and he would personally lead this protest. Finally, the British were convinced that it would be useless to wait for Gandhi's death and therefore, on 4 May, they arrested him.

Even though Gandhi was arrested, the Satyagraha of raiding the Dharasana salt godowns started as planned on 21 May 1931. Before the Satyagraha started, the British government dug moats around the godown and filled them with water. They fenced the area with barbed wire and set up guards. There were riflemen who defended the area, 400 policemen, and six British officers. Groups of Satyagrahis crossed the moat, and as soon as they reached the wire fence, the police would order them to stop. Satyagrahis would try to move ahead, and within minutes, lathis tipped with iron would land on their bodies. The beatings would continue till the last Satyagrahi fell covered in blood. The injured Satyagrahis would be removed on stretchers, and immediately, the next group would move ahead. The same lathis would rain down on them, and they, too, would fall injured. And again, a third …fourth…fifth group would move ahead. This continued for the entire day. Even when they saw their compatriots beaten and bloodied and losing consciousness, it did not prevent the groups from faltering. Nobody went back. Webb Miller, the reporter for the United Press, was present there, and the news that he reported to 1350 newspapers across the world is available to this day.

"The volunteers formed into columns, with their leaders carrying ropes and wire cutters. They advanced slowly for half a mile - a ghostly procession – toward the salt works. The 400 police clutched their clubs, and about twenty-five of them revealed their rifles as the volunteers approached. There were a few cheers, and then the leaders who had ropes attempted to lasso the posts, holding up the barbed wire and intending to uproot them. The police ran up and demanded that they disperse. The volunteers refused. Police charged, swinging their clubs and belabouring the raiders on all sides. The volunteers made no resistance. As the police swung hastily with their sticks, the natives simply dropped in their tracks. Less than 100 yards away, I could hear the dull impact of clubs against bodies. The watching crowds gasped or sometimes cheered as the volunteers crumpled before the police without even raising their arms to ward off the blows. With almost unbelievable meekness, they submitted to the clubbing and were carried away by their comrades who had collected a score of stretchers. As the attacks continued, stretcher-bearers were overworked. Other volunteers joined, using blankets as stretchers for the injured who were falling so fast that the volunteers established a clearing station a hundred yards from the pans. 1 counted forty-two injured lying on the muddy ground and a few others who were unconscious and writhing in pain. After police had driven the raiders back, leaders altered their tactics and started stretching themselves on the ground or sitting in front of the police as closely as they could press to the entanglements. They were warned repeatedly by police, who then struck the men sitting in front of them. The volunteers who were hit simply reeled over on the ground – without making a cry or an effort to defend themselves. Police also altered their tactics and started dragging the volunteers about 100 yards away to the edge of the ditch, splashing mud everyone nearby."

He later wrote, "In eighteen years of reporting in twenty-two countries, during which I have witnessed innumerable civil disturbances, riots, and rebellions, I have never witnessed such harrowing scenes as at Dharamsala."

Some people like Vitthalbhai Patel (he was the president of the central legislative assembly) and his friends told Irwin that the Dandi March would be more humorous than dangerous. After the Dharasana incident, Vitthalbhai Patel handed over his resignation. He said that all paths leading to mutual understanding between India and Britain have been obstructed. "Today morning, the cruel and heartless manner in which the British treated the nonviolent and passive people, how a government that calls itself civilised can act in such a way, I am unable to understand."

All those who forecasted that the Salt Satyagraha would be a humorous affair themselves became the butt of the joke. Webb Miller took Vitthalbhai Patel's comments all across the world.

There was another protest at the salt works in Wadala, Mumbai. Between fifteen and 20,000 people participated in that protest. The police thrashed many people, and the government started unleashing a string of arrests.

In the year after the protests, Churchill said that the protests and their aftermath had "inflicted such humiliation and defiance as has not been known since the British first trod the soil of India." Overall, Gandhi's salt left the British with a burning sensation.

Gandhi was imprisoned, as was Nehru. Nehru said to Gandhi, "May I congratulate you on the new India you have created with your magic touch! What the future brings, I know not, but the past has made life worth living, and our prosaic existence has developed something of the epic greatness in it."

There is a saying –*boond se gayi, houd se nahi ati* – once something is lost, it does not return even with great efforts. The British empire lost face because of Gandhi's lump of salt, and it was never recovered from the humiliation. Gandhi not only tried to bring those at the periphery within the margins but at the centre of the struggle. Those who lived outside the village boundaries, the *Shudras* and *Atishudras*, tried all their lives to give them respect. Through his various protests, he tried to bring consciousness to this 'unconscious' mass of people. He tried to increase their participation, their self-awareness, and self-respect. He brought women out of their homes through the protests and made them aware of their strength. Who else participated in such large numbers in the Salt Satyagraha? Wasn't it the participation of the repressed and marginalised people? Those who kept singing praises of 'who can get independence without battle' were not so naïve as to not understand that participation in the freedom struggle was bound to lead to demand for a share in power after freedom. The RSS was absent in the freedom struggle, Hindu Mahasabha was absent, and Hindutvawadis were absent because it was dangerous for them if independence was procured under the leadership of Gandhi. Would they ever help in the fight or participate in a battle, fully knowing that they would lose their caste supremacy in doing so? Gandhi stood like a villain between them and their authoritative access to power, so it was impertinent for them to get rid of him. It should not surprise anybody if they heard the bells tolling for them even louder after the unprecedented success of Gandhi's Salt *Satyagraha*.

CHAPTER 10

THE WEALTH OF THE FAKIR

What did Gandhi have? Neither power nor wealth nor personal property and yet he was responsible for meeting the requirements of the huge movement. He was, after all, the main actor in this movement and in the role of a father figure. Therefore, he was responsible for meeting the requirements of resources for which the movement depended on him. Where would the poor, naked fakir get money from? Even though he did not have any wealth, he certainly ruled over the hearts of the common people. How can one forget this? This 'ruler' held the key that opened the safe boxes in the hearts of the common people, and from there, he met the wealth to skillfully run his movement.

Wherever Gandhi went, people spontaneously welcomed him and offered him gifts such as bouquets, flower garlands, shawls, and scrolls of honour. Gandhi tried to explain to them not what a waste of money this was and later tried to request them to abstain from such gift-giving, but in vain. He said that their love was enough for him. But he could not stop the tide of material gifts that people brought him as a sign of their love. Whenever Gandhi could not stop something, instead of grumbling or expressing anger, he would try to give it a 'beautiful turn.' In this case, too, he found a new way out. His solution was '*aam kea am guthliyon ke daam*' – having his cake and eating it too!

He started to publicly auction whatever gifts were offered to him in programmes. Flowers, garlands, bouquets, shawls, coconuts, scrolls – everything was up for auction. People looked forward to gifting something because Gandhi had taught them to give, and on top of that, the gift ceremonies were always organised in public, which increased the respect of the giver.

After flowers and garlands were offered to him in a public programme, Gandhi would say from the stage, "I can't see any small child in this place, so what am I to do with these flowers and garlands? Would someone like to buy these?" Immediately, there would be a competition amongst those present to make the purchase. Gandhi himself conducted the auction. He would open the bid for the garlands, and people would increase the bid. Sometimes, a garland would go for Rs.30 and at other times for Rs.300. Once somebody gifted him lemons from his fields, and Gandhi extracted a good price for them. In another meeting, somebody gifted a jewellery box. He said, "Ba and I have never worn jewels, and therefore, there is no question of our owning any jewellery. What use is this jewellery box for me? Would someone like to take it?" Immediately, the auction started. The bid rose up to Rs 300, but Gandhi said he wanted more money. The competition increased, as did the price. Sometimes, in the middle of such auctions, he would say, 'I got Rs.1000 for a similar box.' People would understand, and someone would take the box for a thousand rupees. In this way, a jewellery box would become a treasure.

The citizens of Kolkata gave him scrolls of honour in heavy boxes. All of them were auctioned. At that time, he said, "I auction these things, but this does not mean that I disrespect your love and your feelings. I am not travelling with trunks, so how would I carry these things? And suppose I did take these, where would I keep them? The ashram does not have a place for such things. What can I do in such circumstances?" Gandhi auctioned lemons for Rs. 10, thread garlands for Rs.201, golden *taklis* for Rs.5000, and jewellery boxes for Rs.1000.

There is a story about a beggar who had spent his entire life begging, but in his entire life, he had never given away anything. He knew how to ask but not to give. He filled his house with grains, but he was not satisfied. He keeps begging. He wants more … and more. His greed is endless. God becomes worried about his greed. One day, God comes in the garb of a beggar and, stands at his doorstep and begs, "Give alms to the beggar." The beggar is surprised to see a beggar at his doorstep. He explains to the beggar standing at his door, "I am a beggar myself; what can I give you? You better go away!" He tries to get rid of him, abuses him angrily, and even pushes him away physically, but the beggar refuses to leave. It is time for the beggar to go out begging. Finally, in order to get rid of the man at the door, he picks up one single grain from his store and drops it in the bowl of the beggar who leaves at the door. He returns inside and sees something shining on the heap of grains. He is curious. He finds one grain of gold in the heap. He understands what has happened. He had dropped one grain in the bowl, which turned it into gold. If only he had handed over the entire heap to the beggar!

I always feel that Gandhi must have come across this story somewhere, which is why he gave up his entire life and converted his life into 'gold.' In fact, this beggar who had converted his life into gold developed a Midas touch that turned all those whose lives he touched into gold. All his life, this beggar asked for alms, not for himself but for others, for the country, and for the work of the country.

When the philosopher's stone touched iron, it turned into gold. But Gandhi's power was even more than that. Not just iron, but whatever he touched became gold. Men turned to gold, lemons, garlands, flowers, shawls, and scrolls; everything fetched the price of gold. Unless his touch converted the flower into gold, would the flower have fetched the price of gold?

He used to be invited to ground-breaking ceremonies. Naturally, in such programmes, there used to be pans, baskets, hoes, and spades. Whatever Gandhi touched and was later auctioned always fetched the price of gold.

He auctioned things gifted in meetings as part of fundraising, and sometimes he would spread his cloth bag and request people to put in it whatever they could afford. There would be a rush to put things in the bad. Thus, he would find it easy to raise funds in lakhs from amongst the people. Once, he did not know what to use as a begging bowl, he took the hat of a foreign reporter and held it out in front of him to put some. One after he had put in his support, the hat was passed ahead for others to pour in their help. Once, someone put a broken cowrie (*fukti kavdi*) in his bag. Whoever had dropped the cowrie probably did not harbour good intentions. Perhaps the person who dropped the cowrie wanted to tease Gandhi and make fun of his movement. But Gandhi was hardly the one to take things negatively. He looked at the thing positively and praised it in public. Gandhi said, "It appears as if a poor man has given this. He did not have anything other than this cowrie. Thus, it is not a cowrie but the entire savings that he has given away. This cowrie is invaluable because it is the symbol of sacrifice. It is more valuable than gold." Gandi's touch gave such value to the cowrie that it was sold for Rs.111.

Tushar Gandhi tells us how positive outcomes are possible through optimism. Once, a young man brought a gift in an attractive package where Gandhi was staying, and he insisted, "This has to reach Gandhi alone, and Gandhi must remove the gift from the package." Then the young man left. Gandhi came. His colleagues handed over the gift left by the youth. Gandhi removed the packing and looked inside eagerly. There were old and broken shoes and chappals in the box. Nobody doubts that the 'gift' was given to insult Gandhi. Everyone except Gandhi was angry at whoever was trying to insult Gandhi. Gandhi calmly hands over the box to one of his colleagues and instructs him to sell the contents to a cobbler. The shoes and chappels were thus sold, and the money was handed over to Bapu.

In the evening, Bapu narrated the story at the prayer meeting, and the young culprit was amongst those who were sitting before Gandhi. He knew that Gandhi was bound to tell this story that day. He expected Gandhi to be angry. In the end, Gandhi said that the shoes and chappals were sold to a cobbler, and the money that was received was put in the 'Harijan fund.'

Now, the youth gets angry. He stands in the prayer meeting and insists that the money should be handed over to him because he had sent the shoes and chappals. Then Gandhi asks him calmly, "Did you send me the gift?" the youth said, "Yes."

"Then how can you ask these back?" said Gandhi. The youth is frustrated but remains without an answer.

Why should it surprise us that Gandhi made use of broken shoes and chappals sent specifically as a gesture of insult or a broken cowrie for fundraising? Not only was the cowrie sold at the price of gold donated by Gandhi for a public cause, but copper was also sold at the price of gold. It so happened that a group of public-spirited people raised donations for their cause and came to Gandhi for his blessings. Gandhi gave a copper coin as a symbol of his blessings. Immediately, a Gandhi supporter bought the copper coin for Rs.500. The transactions were very interesting indeed! One broken cowrie = Rs.111. One copper coin = Rs.500. A pinch of salt = Rs.525. Indeed, the lump of salt that shook the foundations of the British empire was bound to be of that value!

After Tilak's death, Gandhi announced that he would collect Rs.1 crore in three months for the Tilak Swarajya Fund. There were loud whispers that Gandhi had announced an exceptionally high target to be met in too short a period of time because no one had ever collected such a large amount in such a short time. During Tilak's jubilee, a mere couple of lakhs were collected in the name of 'Chirol Case Fund.' There were many unsavoury controversies that plagued the fund, which led to the coinage of the term '*fund-gund.*' Before the Tilak Memorial Fund, the highest funds collected were for the Victoria Memorial Fund, which had amounted to Rs. 52 lakhs, but that was after the British administration had supported the effort. But what about the Tilak Swarajya Fund? Who supported that? A fakir named Gandhi! Not just a fakir, but according to Winston Churchill, a 'naked' fakir.

A couple of days before the end of the three months, there was a meeting to take stock of the amounts collected. The collection fell short of the target by a few lakhs. Did that make a difference? But the fakir issused a *farmaan*. He announced that if, by the end of three months, the target amount was not collected, then he would return the amounts to individual donors. His colleagues tried to reason with him. But it would be unlike Gandhi to listen to sage advice. By the end of the given time period, it was not one crore, but one crore and fifteen lakhs were collected. Out of this, the fifteen lakhs was in excess of the target, but the fakir did not utter a word about returning this excess amount to the donors.

The entire British administration's support could not ensure that the Victoria Memorial Fund would go beyond Rs. 52 lakhs, and Gandhi collected one crore fourteen lakhs in the name of Tilak for the Tilak Swarajya Fund. There is a song in Hindi, "*Sabarmati ke sant tune kar diya kamaal* - Sabarmati's saint, you have performed a miracle!" The saint was a miracle worker when it came to fundraising. Gandhi collected funds many times for many different memorials, including those of the martyr girl Veliamma, Gokhale, Lala Lajpatrai, Deshbandhu Chittaranjan Das, C.F Andrews and those who died in Jallianwala Bagh. While collecting the fund in memory of the victims of the Jallianwala Bagh, he announced that if the fund was not collected in the given time, then he would sell his ashram and donate whatever else he could. Gandhi's 'threat' had the effect that we expected.

The strategies, tactics, devices and methods that Gandhi employed to collect funds appear imaginative and invoke respect along with wonder. Once, some tickets were sold for his speech, and the amount was donated to the Deshbandu Memorial Fund. The 'God is truth' speech was recorded. He gave permission to a gramophone company to sell it. In half an hour, he got sixty-five thousand rupees, which he gave to the fund.

Gandhi used to charge for his signature. Those who wanted his autograph had to pay Rs. 5, and even those who donated thousands of rupees to him were not exempted from this rule. Once, he granted a group of students two meetings for a meeting and ended up talking with them for ten. He increased the cost of his signature to cover the loss of the extra time. The students happily gave the amount that Gandhi wanted, and two students gave the rings they were wearing to their fingers. Any pretext would suffice for Gandhi to increase the cost of his signature. The cost increased in the case of the students because they were given more time than he had initially intended for them. Once, a Tamilian businessman wanted his signature in Tamil, and Gandhi doubled the cost of the signature. Gandhi had learned Tamil in South Africa, and he agreed to the demand of the businessman, saying, "I will take double the amount for it." The businessman said that he did not have the money immediately. Gandhi was adamant. He was a banana, after all. "Okay, let it be on loan. I trust you." The businessman gave the amount and also gave the ring on his finger. On this, Pandit Jawaharlal Nehru, who was present, said in jest, "I had heard that the Tamil Chettiyars are the most astute traders."

On this, the Tamil trader replied, "Sir, no one knows how to empty people's pockets better than Mahatmaji. I confess I have lost."

Gandhi said, "No! You have done a profitable deal with me. You are taking the blessings of the poor with you."

The trader touched Gandhi's feet and said, "Your blessings are enough for me."

What the trader had said was not wrong. It was not possible for anyone to empty the pockets of others as much as Gandhi. A doctor treats patients and charges fees for that. Is this not the norm? Or is it the norm that the doctor should pay the patient for examining him? Once, a doctor who was also a friend came to know that Gandhi was unwell and paid him a visit. He was about to leave when Gandhi said in jest, "You are leaving without paying the fees for examining me! Where are my fees?" The doctor had not expected to charge Gandhi his fees. He took his wallet out of his pocket and emptied it into Gandhi's hands. It must be a rare occasion when a doctor pays to examine a patient. But everything was extraordinary about Gandhi, and how could the rules of this world apply to him?

A devotee once told Gandhi, "If you come to my house, I will give you Rs.116 for every minute." Gandhi spent two minutes at his house, and in that time, he extracted Rs.232 for the national cause. Gandhi used to officiate as a priest in the marriages that took place in his ashram. He never accepted any money for himself, but sometimes he would ask for contributions to the Harijan Fund. Once, he officiated as a priest and requested Rs.5000 to construct a well for Harijans, and it was given happily.

Gandhi was the name of a charm, but on whom did this charm work? Once, a murderer who had never met Gandhi was condemned to death. Before being hanged, he was asked to state his last wish. He stated that his last wish was that the Rs.100, which he had deposited in the prison, would be given to Gandhiji for use in the national cause. Another time, when Gandhi was in Lucknow for the Congress session, a woman came to him, and she removed her golden bangles and all the gold jewellery that she was wearing and handed them over to Gandhi. The jewels weighed at least twenty-five to thirty tolas. Gandhi said to her, "Daughter, why are you giving away this jewellery?"

On this, she quickly replied, "Baba, what did you do? You called me 'daughter'! Now, the daughter of Gandhi will not sit in a brothel." The woman was a prostitute. Her life changed completely when Gandhi called her 'daughter.'

Whether it was a murderer, a prostitute, or others who could not physically participate in the national struggle, Gandhi ensured that they participated mentally and monetarily through their donations. How many levels of people's hearts did Gandhi touch?

A group of people who had collected some money on the occasion of Gandhi's birthday wanted to hand it over to Gandhi. Gandhi had a terrible cough, cold, and flu and was suffering, but he still agreed to join the programme. When Vallabhbhai Patel came to pick him up, he was suffering from a massive coughing spell. Vallabhbhai was disturbed by Gandhi's ill health, but he covered it with jest: "There is no end to your greed. Even if you are dying, you will get up and come where you can pick up some money. If you had taken care of your cough in the same manner, then everything else would have fallen in line, but you would hardly have listened."

Sardar Vallabhbhai Patel was asked to speak in the programme. He was still disturbed, angry and disconcerted. He did not like that Gandhi attended the programme in spite of being ill. He said, "Is it my birthday that I should speak?" he further said, "It is a great injustice that he wants to collect the money, and I have to speak. This old man is so ill, but still, he has come to take your money from you. Take some pity on him and let him rest."

Gandhi did not have a house to call his own. He did not have a property to call his own. He did not have a family of his own. He did not have a personal life of his own. He did not agree with the difference between personal and public. Since his days in South Africa, Gandhi had stayed in Ashrams. His Ashrams do not have less than 200-300 people, from different castes, creeds, colours and countries. It is not as if they are all related to him by blood. Most of them are related to him 'beyond blood.' Except for a couple of decades in his life, this man lived nearly fifty years in Ashrams or in prisons or had been travelling.

Throughout his life, he went around with a bowl of begging, not for himself but for the country. People responded by willingly contributing whatever they could, and he was satisfied with whatever was given to him.

Who would bear hatred to the one who had always loved everyone and forgiven even his enemies? And why would they go to the extent of killing him? Was it because Gandhi worked against their 'racism'?

The Hindutvavadi assassins have fabricated some justifications for Gandhi's murder, but the real reason lies elsewhere – they knew that Gandhi posed a challenge to racist and caste-based supremacy, and there was no other way for his opponents except to kill him. They feared that the golden touch of Gandhi's thoughts would defeat them, and the act of murder was born of this fear of defeat. This is the truth, no matter what Nathuram spouts.

CHAPTER 11

THE SPELL CAST BY GANDHI

There were many contemporaries who said Gandhi did not have logic, but he certainly had the magic. Gandhi cast a spell on the common people. Well-read people, and especially Hindutvawadis, would declare, "The public is gullible, and therefore they follow Gandhi." It is the favoured principle of the well-read and well-to-do (or rather well-read and half-baked) that when the public is not with them, then the public is considered ignorant, illiterate, foolish and gullible. This was pronounced in those times, and even today, it is pronounced with vigour. But then one realises that the people in Gandhi's inner circle were far from illiterate, ignorant and gullible. And yet they too were under the spell of Gandhi's magic – what was the logic to this?

Hardly anyone has enjoyed the great success that Gandhi had in collecting different types of people around him, talented people who belonged to different professions, maintaining contact with them and using their talents to achieve his goals. These people were totally unlike each other, and further, they were not carbon copies or, in today's language, the photocopies of Gandhi. Each one had an independent talent, independent perspective and independent ideology. Which rules, chemistry or magic, brought together these constellations in the sky called Gandhi?

Motilal Nehru had little patience for Gandhi's spirituality and did not believe in God at all. He had told Gandhi in clear terms that, at least in this birth, he did not have any faith in God. And yet he said that Gandhi-the-spiritual easily defeated them in the political arena.

The personal sacrifice, commitment and patriotism of Chittaranjan Das were immense. And yet he felt that the same qualities were present in Gandhiji in far greater quantities. A person like Vinoba was equally attracted to the revolutionary zeal of Bengal and the peace of the Himalayas. He left home with that passion and met Gandhi on the way. Vinoba said, "Providence took me to Gandhi, and I found in him not only the peace of the Himalayas but also the burning fervour of revolution, which is so typical of Bengal." The Vinoba who wandered in search of revolution and peace was calmed before Gandhi. Vinoba saw Gandhi as an amalgamation of the fruits of ancient traditions and the seeds of new traditions. He is enchanted by the unity between his inner and outer selves.

Maulana Azad is a deeply spiritual thinker and cultural representative of Gandhi's oriental traditions. Pandit Nehru said that Gandhi brought together the meeting of personalities who were distinct from each other. "Our backgrounds, our lifestyles and our thoughts were all different, but we were brought together for a common goal by a leader whose vision was different from our vision and whom we considered a grand and noble hero." Nehru was a dreamy leader who was impacted by socialist thoughts and dreamt of the Industrial Revolution through big industries; Gandhi dreamt of India's development through small village industries and shared the vision with others. Vallabhbhai Patel was quite different. He was a lawyer in Ahmedabad and joked about Gandhi's politics in the bar room in his free time. Even though he was trapped in Gandhi's charisma, in the end, he committed to Gandhi. He saw in Gandi, a political leader who not only talked but also acted. Dr. Rajendra Prasad, Sarojini Naidu, Rajaji, Acharya Kripalani, Khan Abdul Gafar Khan, Mahadevbhai Desai, and the list is very long, who were all shining stars in Gandhi's firmament. All of them were talented, not only highly educated but men with great intellectual prowess, and they were in love with Gandhi and affected by him. Not only in the political arena but also people in the industrial sector such as Ghanshyam Das Birla, Ambalal Sarabhai, Jamunalal Bajaj, Dr.Pranjivan Mehta and others who were skilful traders and industrialists were ready to listen to his words.

Rabindranath Tagore and Mahatma Gandhi had different viewpoints, but they were tied together by the threads of love. There is a story about the time when Gandhi was in Tagore's Shanti Niketan. Both of them were walking on the Shanti Niketan premises early in the morning. A beautiful morning made more beautiful by the songs of birds. Rabindranath pointed to the birds and asked Gandhi, "These birds who sing sweetly, their chirping, their music – do these have any place in your philosophical vision?"

Gandhi replied, "You are a poet, it is natural for you to desire the sweet music of the birds. But my worries are different. These birds should get food and water. They must eat and drink. If they sleep at night then they can sing in the morning. I worry about their previous night." The perspectives were different, but they were both tied together by the bonds of love.

In his laboratory named 'ashram', there were many eminent social scientists. Gandhi attracted Mamasaheb Phadke who was adept at making bombs, but under Gandhi's guidance, he left his old path of violence and started serving the Harijans. Haren Mehta of Sabarmati Ashram used to eat fifty-five rotis at every meal. He would get upset if there was one roti less. "Are you going to starve me to death?" and if he was given one roti more, then he would shout, "Do you consider me a demon like Bakasur?"

Bhansali was an entirely different type of person. He would only listen to Gandhi. He started a *moun vrat* – maintaining continuous silence – which was broken due to some reason. As a punishment, he sewed his mouth with a copper wire. He would take in liquids through a pipe from a corner of his mouth and lived thereon.

The number of food experiments in the ashram was innumerable. One of Bapu's associates said, "It was recently reported that grass had plenty of vitamins. Fortunately, the discovery was not made when Gandhiji was in the ashram, for then he would have decided to wind up the kitchen and ask us to graze on the lawn." The people in the ashram were of different talents and different types, but they were even enthralled by the name Gandhi. What power did this man have? The others were pulled towards him, and as moths leap towards flames, they leapt towards him.

It did not only happen in India, but it happened with people across the world. Things were not different in South Africa. People kept coming to him and joining him, and the bonds grew stronger over the years. Nothing came between the creation of the bonds – caste, religion, race, language, country, colour, gender – and Gandhi did not allow any of these to enter the relationship. He suffered greatly in South Africa. He was beaten, insulted as 'coolie barrister' at every step. While travelling in first class, he was thrown out of the train on the platform with his luggage. He was insulted as coolie barrister because he wore a turban to court. The barber refused to shave him, so he shaved and became the butt of barbs. 'Did the rats nibble your hair?' He was not allowed in hotels because of his dark skin. He was kicked out because he insisted on sitting in a horse buggy with the Whites.

On returning to South Africa from India, a crowd of Whites attacked him. He suffered abuse, insults and beatings but did not express hatred towards the Whites, nor did he detest them. Thus, Whites like Henry Polak and later his wife Millie Polak, Albert West, Herman Kallenbach, Sonja Schlesin, A.W. Baker, the Quaker Michael Coates, police superintendent Richard Alexander and others fell in love with Gandhi. The first two biographies of Gandhi were written by Whites. Reverend Joseph Doke and Henry Polak were the two biographers.

"If someone does a favour in return for a favour done to him, then this is a mere transaction, something done by thieves and dacoits as well.

Humaneness abhors the thoughts of profit and loss." These were not mere words, but Gandhi imbibed every syllable deep within himself, and therefore, compassion trickled into his behaviour throughout his lifetime. In South Africa, this 'unwanted guest' created many problems and difficulties for General Smuts. He could not understand what to do with this troublemaker. A small, ordinary-looking Indian lawyer, a coolie barrier opposes us, and we are unable to suppress the opposition? Smuts knew how to take care of violent uprisings, but Gandhi discovered a new weapon, 'passive resistance', which he did not know how to face. He tried to repress Gandhi using the regular tactics. But many times, these tactics boomeranged on him. He could not understand how to handle these people who were ready to undergo any suffering, physical hardships and miseries. Smuts' secretary told Gandhi, "I do not like your people and do not care to assist them at all. But what am I to do? You help us in our days of need. How can we lay hands on you? I often wish you took to violence like the English strikers; then we would know at once how to dispose of you. But you will not injure even the enemy... And that is what reduces us to sheer helplessness." Smuts is reduced to a condition of 'love and hate' while fighting against Gandhi. Smuts harbours respect and admiration for Gandhi, but he also feels anger and desperation against him.

Sarvapelli Radhakrishnan edited a volume of Gandhi's life and works on the occasion of his seventieth birthday. "I must frankly confess that his (Gandhi's) activities at that time were very trying to me." This is the same 'trying Gandhi' who was in jail during the Quit India Movement, and there was violence outside. The British government tried to spread the slanderous propaganda that Gandhi was responsible for the violence and encouraging it. General Smuts was exasperated at his government's stance, and openly stated in a press conference, "It is foolish to call Mahatma Gandhi a fifth columnist. He is a great man. He should be counted amongst the great men in the world."

There is no doubt that Gandhi had a huge circle of friends, but there is nothing extraordinary about that. Rather, his capacity to convert the opponent into a friend was unbelievable. While in prison in South Africa, Gandhi made a pair of sandals for Smuts, which he gave him. Upon this, Smuts said, "I may feel I am not worthy to stand in the shoes of so great a man… it was my fate to be the antagonist of a man for whom, even then, I had the highest respect." The 'love and hate' relationship fully changed to love.

Mir Alam, who was present in the movement in South Africa, is a *pathan* with some misunderstandings about Gandhi and tries to kill him. Gandhi goes for self-registration, and Mir Alam and other *pathans* mount a deadly attack on him. Gandhi loses consciousness and falls down. The *pathan* attackers take him for dead, and they make good their escape. Gandhi regains consciousness and enquires about Mir Alam. He comes to know that the police have caught him and immediately sends a message to the police to let him go. He does not register any complaints against the attackers. Over time, the same Mir Alam confesses his mistake and joins Gandhi's movement. In one public meeting, Mir Alam learned that there was an attack planned on Gandhi. He roars, "Whoever attacks Gandhi will fall victim to my knife."

Gandhi calls him close and tries to explain, "Nobody will do anything to me."

He replies, "You are a Fakirbaba! You don't understand anything. I know everybody. I will not tolerate anyone raising his hand against you. I will not stop till I kill the person."

The same Mir Alam who had tried to murder Gandhi was now in the role of his saviour.

Gandhi had the magical power of immediately befriending a person so that the person would become committed to him. He wielded the amazing skill of converting an enemy into a friend, pulling opponents to his side. It took Gandhi only five hours to befriend Henry Polak. Mahadevbhai Desai became devoted to him in just three or four meetings. V.S. Aiyyar melted when he met Gandhi and became a strong follower. Kakasaheb Kalelkar met Gandhi at Rabindranath Tagore's Shanti Niketan and became a lifelong disciple. When Henry Polak's fiancée Millie Polak reached South Africa, Gandhi accompanied Henry to receive her at the station. In the very first meeting, she notes that he had "the kindest eyes in the world, which seemed to light up from within when he spoke." In 1931, Millie wrote a book on Gandhi called 'Mister Gandhi – The Man', in which she wrote about a little-known incident. Gandhi had alighted from the stage after a meeting when a man took him aside. They both walked away together, talking to each other. After this, the man gave Gandhi a bundle and left. Millie saw this and asked Gandhi (who was called Bhai in South Africa), "Who was this man?"

Bhai answered calmly, "He had come to kill me. After our conversation, he has changed his mind." Millie said, "And what was in the bundle?" Bhai replied, "It is his revolver." Millie's heart skipped a beat. She said, "Why didn't you get him arrested?" Bhai laughed and said, "He would have looked for another opportunity… As it is, he will now be my friend."

A man comes to kill Gandhi; he is taken aside by Gandhi. He has a revolver. What could Gandhi have spoken which made him hand over the revolver to Gandhi? To the extent that leaving aside the thoughts of murder sows the seeds of friendship in his heart? It seems totally unbelievable! In all these happenings, there appears to be less logic and more magic.

Hermann Kallenbach and Gandhi's friendship is the friendship of people on two opposite poles. Gandhi is opposed to racism; he is fighting against it in the court of law. Kallenbach subscribed to racist theories. Gandhi was a barrister, and Kallenbach an architect. Gandhi is Indian, and the latter is German. Gandhi was Hindu and a Jew. Gandhi was on a journey to simplicity while he was a carefree person given to an expensive lifestyle and extravagant spending. But he came in contact with Gandhi and changed so drastically that it was astonishing. He got entangled with Gandhi and simultaneously with the movement started by Gandhi. Kallenbach remained present in every public meeting addressed by Gandhi. Whether it is a court case, Gandhi's imprisonment or his release from prison – Kallenbach changed so much in contact with Gandhi that he would laugh and say, "I was covered with racism, but today, if I see a dirty Indian child crying, I lift him up."

This German friend of Gandhi bought 1100 acres of land for the Tolstoy farm. The same Hermann Kallenbach bought a new car to fetch Gandhi after his release from prison. It is different that Gandhi did not sit in it and made him return the car. Kallenbach had a great love for binoculars. There were many arguments with Gandhi over this once they were sailing in a ship when this argument began.

"Instead of arguing over these binoculars, why don't we throw them in the sea?" said Gandhi.

Upon this, Kallenbach said, "Throw them away!"

And Gandhi really threw away the binoculars into the sea without a change in expression. In Gandhi's ashram, Hermann was called 'Hanuman kaka." He was Hanuman, and Gandhi was Ram.

We see that whether it was South Africa or India, wherever Gandhi went, he helped people blossom. Winston Churchill might have harboured anger against Gandhi and taunted him as a 'naked fakir' but his niece, the famous artist Ms Clair Sheridan, made a bust-sized statue of Gandhi with great reverence and said, "Something very big, very important had happened in my life, a turning point in fact, for knowing 'the Great Little Mahatma' wrought a change in me. It was as though my whole nature underwent a metamorphosis." Thus, Churchill receives a rebuttal in his own home.

Gandhi was fighting against the British empire, and an integral part of the empire was England's Royal Navy, led by Admiral Slade. Admiral Slade's daughter Madeleine Slade changes over to Gandhi's side. This family is close to Winston Churchill. This, too, is a rebuttal from within the family for Churchill. It is astonishing to learn about the great sacrifices this woman made by leaving behind her luxurious lifestyle and her palace-like home to join Gandhi in his ashram. Living simply, learning to spin thread on the wheel, sleeping on mats instead of on soft beds, giving up meat with the full knowledge that it is not allowed in Gandhi's ashram and adopting vegetarianism – these are the difficult tests she passed before being accepted in Gandhi's ashram. Gandhi puts her to work as soon as she joins the ashram – the work of cleaning toilets. The daughter of the British admiral leaves her palace, joins Gandhi's ashram, and cleans the toilets as instructed by Gandhi with a smiling face, without complaints. Where does Gandhi get this power?

When Gandhi faced his first trial in India, the atmosphere in the court was worth seeing. The accused is in the witness box, and the English judge is bowing in respect before the accused. The scene was as if the accused were the judge and the English judge were facing trial. At the beginning of the matter, the judge said to the accused, "Even those who differ from you in politics look upon you as a man of high ideals and of noble and of even saintly life." Who said this? An English judge. And who does he say this about? About Gandhi, who stands before him as an accused.

Gandhi is sentenced to six years in prison.

Gandhi comes to court as an accused person, yet the court stands with respect. Now, he is convicted and sentenced to six years imprisonment. He is no longer just an accused but a convicted offender. Yet, when the court rose once again, Gandhi was shown respect by the entire court.

Why do those against whom he fights treat him liberally?

How does Gandhi achieve this seemingly impossible feat? His opponents would say that Gandhi does not have logic, only magic; could that be true? Was this Gandhi's 'black' magic?

When the courts of the British Empire treat him with such respect, would the prisons be any different? Even though the prisons belong to the British?

Gandhi was about to be set free from imprisonment in Aga Khan Palace. Before that, the Jail Superintendent Mr. Ardesir Kateli, came to Gandhi and said, "Tomorrow morning, you will be released; I will be standing in my uniform as an officer. Therefore, I have come now to take your blessings." After the morning prayers, Kateli hands over a gift of Rs. 75 to Gandhiji and said, "You will be seventy-five years in a few days. At that time you will get many gifts. But let my gift be the first one." Where was he the jailor and where was his prisoner? The walls between the jailor and the prisoner had completely dissolved. How did Gandhi get the power to dissolve walls?

The wife of the Jail's Inspector General makes a different request to Gandhi. She comes to bid farewell to Gandhi and says, "Gandhiji, the next time you come to this jail, please inform me beforehand so that my husband can go on leave."

In this prison, Bapu had seen the death of Ba, and he also shouldered the bier of Mahadev Desai, a person from whom he expected that he would conduct his funeral.

Gandhi might have won over the entire world; he might have created a place in the hearts of his enemies, won over the Zionist German Jew Kallenbach, converted his would-be assassin Mir Kasim into his bodyguard, the English judge in court might have bowed before him, he might have blurred the line between the jailor and the prisoner, but he could not win over the Hindutvawadis of his own country.

Dharmavir Dr. Balkrushna Shivram Moonje was considered the *Bheeshma Pitamah* of the Hindu Mahasabha. He represented the Hindu Mahasabha twice in the round table conferences. He was the medical officer during the Anglo-Boer war. More than serving the injured, he was more interested in watching the war. When he went to South Africa from India, he accepted the hospitality of barrister Gandhi, who was noted by his biographer Balshastri Hardas. After reaching South Africa from India and after the end of the Boer war before returning to India, he was a guest in Gandhi's house. Balshastri Hardas said Dr Moonje was struck by Gandhi's love for Mussalmans. As a Muslim cook, I was in Gandhiji's house. He was a Muslim *Bhangi*, and he used to move into the house as a member of the household. The doctor was shocked to see this.

It is not easy to guess whether the doctor's shock was due to his being a Muslim or his being a bhangi. There was no chance that the kitchen in Gandhi's household would be unclean simply because the cook was a *bhangi*. This is because Gandhi was extremely careful with regard to cleanliness. There is no chance that the shock arose from the possibility of the Muslim *Bhangi* being a non-vegetarian because Moonje had a reputation for being a great mutton-lover.

The doctor might have tolerated a Muslim, but he could not possibly digest that he was a *bhangi*. Doctor B.S.Moonje could have tolerated the repulsive shock in Gandhi's household at Durban, but Gandhi had brought the repulsive practices of his South African Durban household into Indian politics. He put his loathsome practices on full public display using the Congress stage. He mixed these repulsive practices into the freedom struggle. It was acceptable to have such practices in the house at Durban, but in 1920, Gandhi formalised the repulsive practice in the Congress Session of Nagpur, the doctor's home city.

One should not be surprised that Gandhi, whom the world desired, was abhorred by the extremist elements for what they considered his loathsome practices, and in the end, they 'slayed' him.

CHAPTER 12

HINDUS AND MUSLIMS AGAINST GANDHI

Doctor Moonje had undertaken great efforts to ensure that the Congress session was held at Nagpur in 1920. Doctor Moonje shouldered the main responsibility of organising the annual session, and Dr Hedgewar accepted the responsibility for food arrangements. In reality, before the rise of Gandhi in Indian politics, the line between the Hindu Mahasabha and Congress was a hazy one. It was so hazy that many times, the meetings of Hindu Mahasabha and Congress were held on the same date and venue. But after Gandhi's arrival, this situation changed rapidly, and unfortunately, it changed in the very Nagpur session for which Dr Moonje had put much at stake. Dr Moonje's dream that the session should be presided over by Lokmanya Tilak could not be fulfilled because Tilak expired before the session was held. The president of the session, Vijay Raghavachari, was to make a speech. Before his speech, Gandhi made an appeal that his speech, which was opposed to the civil disobedience movement, should be heard peacefully, but people did not listen to Gandhi. The audience created a great commotion during that speech. People were not ready to hear anything against Gandhi.

In his speech, Jinnah referred to Gandhi not as 'Mahatma Gandhi' but as 'Mister' Gandhi and therefore, people did not allow him to speak at all. Naturally, Dr. Moonje had not undertaken pains for this to happen. There was a crowd larger than ever before. The same loathsome atmosphere that Dr Moonje had seen in Gandhi's household at Durban was now obvious in the session in the form of the Muslim crowd. The crowd of women only increased the 'filth.' In this Congress session, along with the question of Hindu - Muslim the questions of Brahmin versus non-Brahmin and untouchability were also discussed. Those who considered Congress to be a political forum did not like this at all. But they were helpless because they were the ones who had organised this session.

In the Congress session at Pune, Tilak's disciple Shridhar Vitthal Date threatened Justice Ranade and forced him to organise a social conference outside the session premises, and now, with the blessings of Gandhi, the social agenda was back at the top of the Congress agenda. There was a special reference to the workers' movement in this session. Certainly, this was not the agenda for which Dr Moonje, Dr Hedgewar and Dadasaheb Khaparde had insisted on Nagpur as the venue of the session. In this session, Gandhi undertook the collection of Rs. 1 crore for the 'Tilak Swarajya fund.' Tilak's followers, who were full of hatred for Gandhi, could not digest Gandhi's acceptance of Tilak's name.

In 1907, Congress leader and chief of the moderate faction Pherozshah Mehta threw out Dr. Moonje from the premises of his bungalow. Dr Moonje successfully organised the Congress session in Nagpur, but in the end, he must have felt that his vision of Hindutva had been dismissed from the session. He had aimed to have Tilak as the president of the session, but unfortunately, Tilak died. The session happened but without Tilak, and to make matters worse, Gandhi, the upstart, won over the proceedings. In effect, Dr. Moonje's efforts were all in vain – all credit and power went to Gandhi. The organising work of the Nagpur session was done by the Dr Moonje-Hedgewar duo, but eventually, their vision of Hindutva could not prevail. Much to their dislike, the Hindutva ideology followed by Dr Moonje and his colleagues were thrown out, and Gandhi took centre stage as the leader.

The crowd and chaos at Nagpur were unforgettable. Even as the session was in progress, it was amply clear that the very face and nature of Congress was transforming. Caste and class consciousness were losing their tight stranglehold over Congress. The manner in which innumerable castes and communities congregated provided a glimpse into the future course of Congress. This was also the session after which Jinnah moved away from Congress, and the Hindutvawadis distanced themselves as well. In the next five years, they moved away from Congress and formed the Rashtriya Swayamsevak Sangh, which was also in Nagpur - such was the coincidence.

Jinnah's Muslim League was fundamentally opposed to Gandhi and the Congress, just as the RSS was opposed to Gandhi and the Congress. There is little difference in the manner and extent of the opposition posed by the Muslim League and that posed by the Hindu Mahasabha – both opposed Gandhi's leadership tooth and nail. In the Quit India Movement of 1942, the ordinary people of India came together under the leadership of Gandhi, while the Muslim League and the Hindu Mahasabha joined hands to enjoy positions of power. The Muslim League accused Gandhi of favouring the Hindus, while at the same time, the Hindu Mahasabha pronounced him guilty of favouring the Muslims.

Hindutvawadis held Gandhi responsible for the partition, whereas it was Muhammad Ali Jinnah, more than anyone else, who was responsible for demanding partition and eventually creating Pakistan. The strange thing is that the Hindutvawadis are never seen criticising Jinnah. It is not as if the Hindutvawadis do not know the implications of Jinnah's call for 'direct action.' They are very much aware that after this call, the Hindus in Bengal were killed in riots in huge numbers, Hindu women were raped, and Hindu homes were burnt into ashes. We don't see any Hindutvawadis speak out against the tortures heaped on Hindus, or against those responsible for the rapes of Hindu women, for the destruction of Hindu homes. We certainly do not see them seeking revenge against Jinnah, whose call for 'direct action' was at the root of this destruction. Nobody is seen attempting to harm Jinnah, let alone 'slay' him. Is it that those who were baying for Gandhi's blood never felt the slightest anger, hate or disgust towards Jinnah? No anger or hate or abhorrence towards the man who is responsible for the destruction of Hindus on such a massive scale? And yet they felt like heaping the worst criticism on Gandhi, who was trying his best to share the sorrows of Hindus in Noakhali, was putting his life at stake to rehabilitate them, and finally, they felt like slaying him. But why?

There is not the slightest criticism against Jinnah, who was directly responsible for the creation of Pakistan from the Hindutvawadi side. There is not even an attempt to attack him, let alone commit actual murder, but the entire blame for the partition is heaped on Gandhi, and he is condemned to death! In another strange twist, Gandhi is blamed for converting Jinnah into a communal person, and therefore, Jinnah is offered further sympathy. Hindutvawadis never tired of narrating with much admiration how Jinnah protected the statue of Tilak during the riots in Karachi.

Gangadhar Indulkar, a person from the Sangh, wrote a book titled *'Rashtriya Swayamsevak Sangh – Kaal, Aaj ani Udya.'* Dr. Moonje's grandson, R.M. Deshpande, lived and worked in Karachi, and he wanted to leave the place during the partition. Dr. Moonje wrote a private letter to Jinnah, after which Jinnah's private secretary went to the place where Deshpande lived and helped him escape safely to India. When Lal Krishna Advani was the supreme leader of the BJP, he publicly praised Jinnah, and the RSS expressed great outrage. One does not know whether the uproar was true or just a show put only for political ends. Sarsanghachalak Sudarshan, too, had praised Jinnah towards the end of his tenure. BJP government's foreign minister Jaswant Singh wrote a big fat book on Jinnah. What is this inexplicable business about the Hindutvawadis' hate for Gandhi and their love for Jinnah?

Before independence, the two organisations with apparently opposing ideologies, the Muslim League and Hindu Mahasabha, were politically complementary to and supportive of each other. Prof. N.R. Phatak has compared the two organisations and clearly stated that the Hindu Mahasabha was a younger version of the Muslim League and strengthened the League's demand for Pakistan. He further states that the Hindu Mahasabha is the shadow of the Muslim League – '*shuddhi*' and '*sangathan*' in the Hindu Mahasabha are after all the translations of '*tanzeem*' and '*tableegh*' of the Muslim League.

Suppose the Muslim League said that we are first Muslims and then Indians; the Hindu Mahasabha, not to be left behind in this matter, declared that they were first Hindus and then Indians. These two declarations strengthen Prof. Phatak's assertion that the Hindu Mahasabha was the shadow of the Muslim League. The two-nation theory based on which Jinnah demanded Pakistan closely followed the theory of Hindu Nationalism, which Sawarkar proposed in 1937 during the annual session of the Hindu Mahasabha. They were the ones who agreed that there were two nations in one country – the Hindu nation and the Muslim nation – and they were the ones who manufactured uproar against Gandhi when the two nations were actually partitioned. They manufactured an utterly false narrative that Gandhi was responsible for the partition. Their real sorrow was that while Jinnah was successful in creating a Muslim nation, i.e. Pakistan, they were unsuccessful in their attempts to create a Hindu *Rashtra*.

Muslims, by and large, stood behind Jinnah, but Hindus did not stand behind the Hindutvawadis; they stood behind Gandhi firmly. Someday, Hindutvawadis would have to figure out why it was when they were shouting from the rooftops that Gandhi was a Hindu hater, and yet Hindus rallied behind him. The basic pain of the Hindutvawadis is that Gandhi started to embed equality as a part of the freedom struggle. The same Vallabhbhai Patel, whom the Hindutvawadis are praising today for their own narrow reasons, said in the Lok Sabha that Hindu Mahasabha's one faction is not satisfied with Gandhi's assassination was now planning to assassinate Nehru as well. In the same speech, Sardar Patel said, 'They do not only want Hindu Rashtra, they want a Brahmin State.' The ordinary Hindus were conscious of this agenda, and therefore, till Gandhi was alive and even after his death for a long time, they did not follow the Hindutvawadis; this much is clear.

While ushering in the value of equality in the national freedom struggle, Gandhi tried to downplay the hold and impact of the elites on the movement and included a large number of Bahujan in it. He explained the uselessness of creating a nation based on religion, and his stand was vindicated when Pakistan was partitioned a second time. If a nation could survive on the basis of religion alone, then why was Pakistan, a nation for Muslims, forced to undergo a second partition? This is a question that the Hindutvawadis would have to answer, even though they have avoided it thus far. Pakistan, created under the leadership of Jinnah, was partitioned a second time, and there is every possibility of further partitions in the future; by contrast, India, which became free under the leadership of Gandhi, remains united. Democracy continues to function in India. The army has still not given in to the greed of taking over the country, whereas Pakistan has remained under martial law for extended periods. Gandhi carefully cultivated democratic and inclusive values within the freedom struggle, which has served India well. Today, people of various castes and communities are moving forward in different spheres of life. The credit for this, too, goes to Gandhi because he introduced the participation of common people in the freedom struggle.

It is not as if India did not have a history before Gandhi, but the pre-Gandhi history belonged to royal dynasties and their palaces. If the common man in the country got a place in history, it is because of their participation in the freedom struggle, and the credit for that definitely goes to Gandhi.

In reality, there is no difference between the fundamentalism of the Hindus and the Muslims. Both share a common core of bigotry and a commitment to protect the vested interests of the upper class and caste at any cost. Muslims use the slogan 'Islam is in danger', and Hindutvawadis use the cover of caste and religion to further their narrow interests. Indeed, Satan does not remain limited to the Bible; when required, the holy texts of the Hindus and the Muslims are also quoted.

In the mutiny of 1857 called the 'freedom struggle' by Sawarkar, the Badshahs, Rajas, Nawabs, Maulvis, and priests issued a number of calls and *fatwas* for Hindu-Muslim unity. It is not at all clear whether or how this battle was linked to the issues of the common people or to their hopes and aspirations. Kings and emperors, nawabs and princes were in fear of losing their vested interests to the British and, therefore, came together to challenge the latter. They were forced to set aside their casteism, racism and communalism temporarily and join forces. We cannot deny that the Queen of Jhansi Laxmibai is the symbol of our identity, but it is also true that when she said *'meri Jhansi nahi doongi'*, the battle is limited to saving *her* Jhansi - someone is trying to steal her Jhansi, and she is not ready to give it, and the fight is simply between one who is trying to take, and another is not ready to give. Where are the common people in all this?

Under Tilak, the ideological vision underlying the demand for independence was somewhat similar. It was limited to retrieving power from the British and returning it to the hands of the Brahmins. This myopic political vision could not countenance the raising of social issues as part of the freedom struggle – the struggle was only for political freedom – the complications of social questions could be left to be detangled another day. Let the power come to our hands, and we shall deal with it later. Common people know that the time to 'deal with it later' never arrives. The common people who were conversant with the repressions of the British Raj had already undergone the repressions of previous regimes. The only difference is that the British Raj was foreign, while the previous ones were indigenous. Comparatively speaking, the treatment of the British foreigners was of greater equality than that of the native kings. The sun of education had been caged by the native rulers, but under the British Raj, some rays of that sun fell on the bodies of the common people. Therefore, those who wanted social freedom opposed those who aimed at merely political freedom.

After Gandhi entered the freedom struggle, he changed the very definition of 'freedom'. Why do we want freedom, and for whom? - For the first time this question was posed by Gandhi. This question begins to expose the caste and class prejudices of many important persons. Further, he exposes the false dualities embedded in the question of whether social issues should take precedence over political issues. Those who opposed the British for political reasons began to feel that they would rather deal with the British than with Gandhi. The last time an extremist shot at a British in freedom struggle was in 1918. Thereafter, their aim shifted to Gandhi because Gandhi had replaced the British as their enemy number one. It is worth pondering over the fact that Gandhi topped the list of enemies for all three – the Hindutvawadis, the Muslim League and the British.

The accuracy and immediacy with which Gandhi understands his opponents is more than the accuracy and immediacy with which he understands his friends. Therefore, it was obvious that he was bound to get in trouble. Gandhi tied this country together as one, and till today, it remains unbroken. There are continuous efforts to break Gandhi away from the country. If such efforts were successful, then the minute Gandhi separated from the country, the country would break. It is a bitter truth. If the country is to remain united, then Gandhi must remain united with the country.

CHAPTER 13

THE NON-CONFORMIST GANDHI

Gandhi entered Indian politics – a rather clumsy man with a gentle demeanour but one whose impact was intense and revolutionary. He was a perpetual headache for the self-proclaimed 'leaders' who ruled over contemporary social structures - where could they place such a man in their scheme of things? Gandhi delivered the first jolt in November 1917 while chairing a meeting in Gujarat. He tore up the draft resolution of loyalty to the British monarch – a common formality on such occasions. It is not surprising that the moderate faction was adept at passing such resolutions, but even the extremist faction of Congress had never broken this rule. Gandhi did not waste a minute before breaking this tradition. Should he then be called an ultra-extremist? But the explanation he gave would not allow that. He said that such resolutions are not passed even at the conferences organised in England, and as long as people don't declare themselves as rebels, their loyalty should be presumed. The core is as fiery and intense as the exterior is calm and innocent. This tactic was easily understood by the common people but was difficult to accept by the intellectuals. There is a saying in Gandhi's Gujarati – *'bhanya pan ganya nahi,'* which means that the educated are not necessarily wise. This was the situation of educated people regarding Gandhi.. What else can be expected when grassroots workers are not considered intellectuals but the term is reserved for critics?

Gandhi subscribed to the four-fold caste system; Gandhi was a casteist – before making such accusations, one has to answer why the casteist and Manuvadi forces attacked Gandhi all his life to the extent of finally taking his life. How long are accusations going to be made against Gandhi while bypassing this core question? Gandhi's language may appear to be moderate while addressing the issue of casteism, but he is the one who has achieved maximum impact on that issue.

One of my friends is a Gandhian. He went to Konkan and started removing the hides of dead cattle, tanning the hide and sewing shoes. My friend did this work because, as a Gandhian, he felt this was what Gandhi wanted him to do. He even organised a training camp to teach the skills of hiding, tanning and cobbling. He announced through various media that all those who wanted to learn how to remove the skin of dead animals, tan the hides and make shoes out of leather may come and attend the camp. According to him, there were forty-two trainees in that camp, of which only three were young, and the rest thirty-nine were aged, most of them beyond seventy years of age. They had done this work in Konkan, following Gandhi's instructions. The most shocking thing was that all of them were Chittapavan Brahmins. These old men belonged to the times when most political leaders in Maharashtra were Brahmins. A majority of them were barristers. Very few were doctors because being a doctor posed the greatest problem for the Brahmins from the point of view of maintaining their caste purity. Patients could be from any caste, and it would be impure if the shadow of such a patient fell on them, and touching them would certainly lead to a social stigma. Instead of taking the huge risk of such stigma, they avoided practising medicine. Such was the logic of those times when these people of Konkan, and that too Chitapavan Brahmins, on the instructions of Gandhi, started skinning and tanning the hides of dead animals, thereby doing the work of the outcaste Chambhars. We cannot imagine the outcry that must have occurred at the time today. Gandhi had engineered a transgression regarding occupations, which is considered a sin in the four-fold Varna system, which was nothing short of revolutionary. If a shudra transgressed into the occupations of the higher castes, it was punishable by death - Shambhuk studied the Vedas and therefore had to be 'slayed.' Suppose the transgression was committed by a Brahmin; how would he be 'slayed'? After all, the murder of a Brahmin was considered an unforgivable sin. But if a Vaishya like Gandhi is 'slayed' by Brahmins, then it would certainly not be considered a sin.

Many continue to question Gandhi's social contribution without realising that the real answer to that question lies in the fact that he was murdered by the Manuvadis. If Gandhi's untouchability removal campaign started infecting those who had invented untouchability in the first place, we can imagine today what outrage the event must have caused. In Maharashtra, Gandhi was opposed tooth and nail by Brahmins, and yet we cannot forget that there were Brahmins amongst those who suffered by following him - they were beaten, abused by their relatives and close ones and humiliated. Unfortunately, a Brahmin murdered Gandhi, and it has become convenient to overlook the contribution of Brahmins, but that is not the truth. After all, it would be fundamentally wrong to confuse convenience with truth.

Gandhiji used to declare himself a Sanatani Hindu, but we should understand why the Sanatanis

attacked him mercilessly. Vidyavachaspati Atmaram Shastri wrote a letter to Gandhi about the theory of caste. According to him, the lower castes were full of evil from the top of their bodies to their toes. Upon this, Gandhi replied that the upper castes were responsible for every vice that was seen in the lower castes. Thereafter, Gandhi was accused of putting justice on its head, and it was rumoured that if Gandhi's 'Raj' came about, it would lead to the destruction of the Hindu Dharma, and therefore, Hindus should be prepared to oppose him. It was conveniently understood that the attack on Hindu Dharma by Gandhi was an indication of his love for Muslims, and therefore, attacking Gandhi became a priority of the Hindutvavadis. They presented Gandhi's attack on Brahminism as an attack on the Hindu Dharma. They had no alternative but to present him as a Muslim lover in order to show that he was a hater of Hindu Dharma, an enemy of the Hindu Dharma.

For N.B. Khare, a leader of the Hindu Mahasabha, Gandhi was an incarnation of Aurangzeb - when Aurangzeb could not destroy the Hindus, he realised that this task could only be completed as a Hindu and therefore, he took rebirth as Gandhi. Even Shastri, who was so interested in theories, did not raise questions about how Aurangzeb went to heaven after his death and pleaded to convert to Hinduism and how a Hindu God agreed to this religious conversion in order to destroy the 'Swadharma.'

Similarly, the intense Gandhi-hatred of Godse and Apte, who were influenced by the Hindu Mahasabha led by Sawarkar, is not only evident from the brutal assassination which they carried out but also from the memoirs of R.P. Nene who was a member of their 'Hindu Rashtra dal.' When Gandhi arrived at Pune, R.P. Nene went to his prayer meeting and was touched. This became known to Narayan Apte, and he said, 'How can such activists become Sawarkarvadis? If I were present, I would have felt like giving two slaps on the Mahatma's face.' In fact, the fire of his hatred increased in the future to the extent that it could not be extinguished by just two slaps on the Mahatma's face.

It is not as if only those who followed Sawarkar harboured such hatred against Gandhi. Sawarkar's brother Babarao Sawarkar made a connection between Gandhi and Amir Amanullah of Afghanistan. According to him, Gandhi and Amir Amanullah entered into a secret agreement, and Gandhi invited Amir to invade India. In his book 'Hindu Rashtra: Past, Present and Future' he harped on this baseless allegation. He also presents Gandhi's civil disobedience movement as associated with the secret agreement. Further, the suspension of the civil disobedience at Bardoli after the violence at Chauri-Chaura was linked to the purported agreement with Amir. In a bizarre fashion he argues the Muslims in the British army would not have fought against Amanullah at all, and Gandhi would have ensured that the Hindu soldiers and the public remained silent as well. While saying this, he unwittingly gives in that Hindu soldiers and the Hindu public were prone to following Gandhi's directions. Gandhi is anti-Hindu, and yet the Hindus hold on to his directions, and Hindu Mahasabha, Sawarkar, and so-called Hindutvawadis do not hold any sway over the Hindus; the Hindus do not care for them – this much is indirectly conceded by Babarao Sawarkar. The reason presented for the suspension of the civil disobedience movement is that since the British stopped Amanullah in his own country, the plans of invasion could not fructify, and therefore Gandhi suspended the movement under the pretext of the Chauri-Chaura riots. Neither Vinayak Damodar Sawarkar nor any other Hindutvawadi leader ever openly opposed the secret agreement; of course, there was no need for them to do so. They did not want to get in the way of hatred and slander targeted at Gandhi; what other reason could there be for their silence?

Babarao Sawarkar reaches a similar venomous conclusion regarding 'the secret agreement.' 'Gandhi is a bigger sinner than Jaichand who invited Mohammed Ghori and through him got Prithviraj Chauhan removed.' Even here they lose their balance. Jaichand took the help of the outsider Ghori to remove Prithviraj Chauhan, who was from his own religion – how does this compare with the situation under foreign rule in India. Because of their hatred for Gandhi, the British Raj became acceptable to the Sawarkar brothers. Perhaps these are the reasons why the Hindutvawadis opposed the freedom struggle led by Gandhi and extended support to the British.

Gandhi intimately tied the welfare of untouchables, Adivasis, farmers, labourers, workers, and women to this struggle. He instilled the desire for freedom in the villages and awakened the feeling of nationalism within diverse castes, religions, languages and cultures. His new definition of freedom struggle was one in which the freedom of the last person, the most oppressed person, was taken into account. Under Gandhi's leadership, the path of struggle led to equality and fraternity and, therefore, to democratic governance.

The very idea of such freedom was even more foreign to the Hindutvawadis than the British rulers. Therefore, there is nothing surprising if they considered the British rule more acceptable than the freedom struggle under the leadership of Gandhi.

They made it their life's sole mission to paint Gandhi as a Muslim appeaser. The riots after the partition provided a solid rock to build their Gandhi-hatred. We have already considered the speeches of Lokmanya Tilak, delivered in 1918 at Athni, and Sir Syed Ahmed's speech delivered at Lucknow, delivered in 1888. The languages of the two might be distinct, but there is no difference in the significance of the words. In 1930, a grand Muslim conference was held in Mumbai which Jinnah addressed saying, , "We refuse to participate in the movement started by Mr. Gandhi because his movement is not aimed at complete freedom for India but to bring the seven crore Muslims under the supremacy of the Hindu Mahasabha." This is what Jinnah said for Gandhi, and on the other side, the Hindu Mahasabha regards Gandhi as an enemy and is prepared to do away with him. Their refrain is that Gandhi and Gandhi's Congress do not represent the Hindus; it is the Hindu Mahasabha which is the true representative of the Hindu interest. Jinnah asserts that the Muslim League is the sole representative of the Muslims. Who was Gandhi representing? Hindu Mahasabha led the Hindus; Muslims were led by the Muslim League; who was following Gandhi? And why is it that Gandhi, who did not claim any followers, became the targe of curses and abuse?

There was a time during the Khilafat movement when even the Muslims were with Gandhi. Jinnah considered Tilak a nationalist and a sympathiser of Muslims, but he considered Gandhi to be an opponent of the Muslims. Tilak allows separate electorates to Muslims under the

Lucknow pact, but no one accuses Tilak of being a Muslim sympathiser. Not just the Hindutvawadis but even Jinnah praises Tilak, and both abuse Gandhi. B.N. Jog, who has studied the Hindu-Muslim question, said the following about the Lucknow pact, "Tilak did nothing to bring the Muslim community into the national mainstream. Through this pact, they want the community to remain superstitious and self-centred. Through this pact, the Muslims' desire to negotiate was awakened, and the capacity of the Hindus to oppose such desire was obliterated. This pact gave a lot to Hindus and Muslims. The Lucknow pact created the feeling in Hindus that they should give whatever the Muslims desired, leading to terrible outcomes over the next thirty years. This pact was considered a great accident in the history of the country. This pact did not lead to unity amongst Hindus and Muslims, the freedom struggle did not make any headway, and it cannot be denied that this pact laid the foundations for the creation of Pakistan. At best, we can say this pact was not a mistake by Tilak but a lack of political alternatives at the time. But it cannot be denied that the foundations for Pakistan were laid through this pact. If this is so, then why was Gandhi attacked and hounded for partition?

Gandhi is portrayed as a Muslim sympathiser, but Maulana Mohammad Ali said in his speech at Ajmer in 1924, "No matter how pure Gandhi's character is, still through the eyes of my religion it is lower than that of any Muslim, however lowly he might be." In the Lucknow speech in the same year, he used slightly different words, "Yes, I consider the degenerate and lowly Muslim at a higher status than Gandhi, according to my religion and sect." Maulana Muhammad Ali's words, with some changes, could well belong to the Hindutvawadis.

It is quite natural that organisations that support birth-based supremacy, whether Hindus or Muslims, hate Gandhi, who is arraigned against caste-based supremacy. They spread the worst canards against him.

Gandhi was religious, but his religion was not based on hatred for other religions. Gandhi's religion aimed to convert the animal-like behaviour of human beings such that they can be called humans, while others used religion to awaken the dormant beast in humans. In the end, what does 'culture' mean? – a chain of constant and continuous attempts to remove the beast inside humans. Gandhi tried to do this all his life, but the 'disfigurements' hiding behind 'culture' killed him in the end.

CHAPYTER 14

STRUGGLE AGAINST THE SELF

'Day and night the war persists, within and outside, the world and the soul' – these words may have been penned by the great Saint Tukaram in his *abhang*, but it was Gandhi who literally lived through such a war his entire life. There are many who fight and live through external wars, and there are those who struggle internally. It is commonly believed that the two battles are quite distinct; the battlefields are very different from each other, and the soldiers are of very different types. The division is quite clear - external wars pertain to politics and social activism, and internal wars are spiritual in nature. Yet Gandhi was one person who fought both battles simultaneously because he did not believe that there was any fundamental opposition between the two. He saw both as '*abhang*' unbroken, in a continuum with each other. He did not believe that when it came to political or social freedom, one could be prioritised over the other. Similarly, he appears to be reluctant to make a distinction between internal and external. He is not ready to make a division between the private and the public. Not only did he actually live the '*abhang*' of Saint Tukaram, but he was a strong proponent for upholding the continuum in every aspect of life. This is why he remained steadfastly unbroken in his life.

Nearly twenty years of struggle in South Africa and three decades of struggle in India means that he spent half a century of his life in struggle. And this struggle was against an empire on which the sun never sets. This man did not tire. This was not the only struggle; there were many other struggles within this one. The struggles between different castes; there were tensions. His struggles between Hindus and Muslims were undeniably present. There were battles against traditions, customs, harmful rites and rituals. These battles were visible. But he fought other battles against himself. This desperate battle was not less important than the others.

Henry Polak forced Gandhi to carry Ruskin's *Unto this Last* to read during the twenty-four hours of travel between Johannesburg and Durban in South Africa. Before this, hundreds of thousands of people have read this book. Perhaps they liked it as much as Gandhi did and it must have generated many discussions. But Gandhi read the book, liked it, and adopted it in order to live by it. It is understandable if one likes a vision, but to like a vision does not necessarily mean living the vision. Gandhi started to implement the core messages of the book in his life - one's welfare is the welfare of all, the value of the service offered by a lawyer is the same as that offered by a barber, the life of bread labour led by the simple farmer is the true life. Henry Polak, who had offered the book without giving too much thought to it as reading material for a journey, was deeply astonished. Gandhi had started the journey of life according to the book given to be read in a journey.

'The welfare of all is one's own welfare' – the *sutra* became embedded deeply in Gandhi. Therefore, the journey of the next fifty years was devoted to the welfare of society. At one point Gandhi could no longer be separated from society; he had become one with it. This oneness did not allow him to tire because he was not doing something apart from living his own life. The ease in the act of breathing was the ease with which he acted for society. In the half-century of political life, Gandhi may have won some battles and lost others, but he never tired. Why? The answer lies in that he completely immersed himself in society and sought oneness with it.

Mohandas decided to return from South Africa to India in October 1901. He has assured his colleagues there that he would return if needed. A party is planned to bid him farewell. He is given gifts. People are giving him a lot of expensive items – silver, gold, diamonds, and precious stones. Here, his battle with himself begins. How could he refuse the gifts that were being offered? Would refusal mean humiliating the affection of the giver? Such humiliation could not be right. And yet, to what extent could the acceptance of such gifts be right? Having accepted the principle of simple living, accepting such gifts, keeping them and collecting them would be breaking the principle. This would be hurting oneself. In this battle with himself, he decides to return all the gifts. The feelings of the giver should not be hurt, and at the same time, one's principles should be upheld and respected. There is a third aspect in this matter – that of the family. The gifts are given not just to Gandhi but also to his family. There are gifts for Kasturba and their sons. More or less, the owner of the gifts is not Gandhi alone but his family members as well. He immediately and easily convinces Harilal and Manilal, but it is not easy to convince Kasturba.

"I don't agree with this. We should not refuse the gifts that friends have given us with so much love," Kasturba is adamant.

"But accepting such gifts is immoral for social work,"

"I don't feel so."

"What are you going to do with these things?" Gandhi.

"I will keep them safe for my daughters-in-law," Kasturba argues.

The sons who are already on Gandhi's side say aloud, "We don't want such gifts."

Kasturba burns in the humiliation of being left alone. In the end, Gandhi is victorious.

It is not easy to fight with oneself or with one's family members. Gandhi fought these battles continuously. He did not allow words like non-possession and non-attachment to become hollow but absorbed and digested them in his blood, flesh and bones. Gandhi's external battles were visible, but the continuously on-going internal battles were largely ignored.

Gandhi is 77 years old. The country has achieved independence. The credit goes to Gandhi's leadership. But this man is not ready to take the credit for freedom. When the celebrations of independence are going on, he is in an unknown village of Bengal. He is concerned with wiping the tears of riot victims, giving them relief from pain. Delhi has invited people to participate in the celebrations. It was not a formal invitation but one extended from the heart. He said, "When thousands of my countrymen are killing each other, how can there be celebrations?" Where and how do this detachment and oneness, this total empathy with the afflicted, come from? When he is roaming barefoot in the villages of Bengal, the world's news reporters are desperately waiting to get his response to the Declaration of Independence. All day long, these people surround him, trying to evince a statement, but Gandhi does not give in. Many of them are tired and leave. However, the representative of BBC remains; he is resolute about not moving away without Gandhi's response. Finally, Gandhi said to him, "Forget that I know English," and avoided him. Where does such detachment and disinterest come from?

There is every possibility of bitterness, resentment and hostility at the end of a struggle over fifty years because while you give everything, your colleagues keep their cards close to their chests. You trust someone, but they betray your trust. You have expectations that are not met. You are humiliated and insulted many times, and that too by people for whose welfare you are working. In the riots after independence, Gandhi faced such insult at every step. If he went here to stop riots, he was told to go to 'their' side. If he went there, he was told to go to the Himalayas. Such humiliation would have stopped one in their tracks. One could have said, "Do what you want to do! Die if you want to kill each other!" But Gandhi did not do so. Instead, when asked to go to the Himalayas, he replies calmly and without any anger, "I would have gone to the Himalayas if I felt that my God resides there. But my God is in you. How can I leave this God and go to the Himalayas?" Where does this attitude come from? How does it come?

Would it have mattered to Gandhi if he had not put his life at stake to stop the riots? But he immersed himself in society and could not separate himself from people's joys and sorrows. This was not his political 'artificiality' but his innermost spontaneity, which he has achieved through his lifelong internal and external battles. Gandhi could smile till the end of his life with the innocence of a small child. He could retain his sweetness. Small children can laugh with abandon because they do not maintain a distinction between the inner self and the external appearances. There is no deception in their lives, but with age, there comes an increasing distance between the inner and the outer. Deception starts creeping in. Men who are considered 'great' by usual standards are definitely afflicted by such deception. This is why they have to struggle greatly to maintain their image. We don't see this happening with Gandhi because he was not only great by the usual standards but by the unusual standards as well. Similarly, it is usual to respond to hatred, humiliation, and animosity in similar terms. To respond according to how a person responds to us is acting according to usual standards, but to respond with compassion no matter how the other person acts towards us is to act according to unusual standards. By that measure, Gandhi was an unusual man.

There were four attacks on Gandhi's life in South Africa. In India, too, he was attacked, but he never registered offence against the attackers. On the contrary, he requested that no offence be registered against them and that they be forgiven. When he was made to appear before the court as an offender, he would ask the magistrate to order the maximum punishment against him. He never asked for a reduction in sentence and certainly never for a waiver of punishment. He accepted his sentence joyfully and underwent full punishment. And yet he is a coward, according to the Hindutvavadis, and the one who apologised again and again to escape punishment is considered 'Veer' or Brave. He did not stop his work out of fear for his life or any other fear, nor did he accept a security force for his personal safety. "I am going to live 125 years," Gandhi would say. His detractors would openly reply, "Who is going to allow you to live for so long?" and yet Gandhi did not accept security teams. Instead, he refused every time security was offered to him.

The extent, scale and perseverance of Gandhi's work are astonishing. This man worked continuously for more than fifty years. Meetings, prayer meetings, rallies, marches, walking tours, travel, imprisonment, struggles, and fasts all became an inseparable part of his life. On top of that, he ran an ashram, set up institutions for constructive work, found the proper persons to run the institutions and put them to work, and introduced programmes for them – he performed the task of 'weaving' that is required to achieve all this, all through his life. His vast correspondence leaves us speechless. Gandhi is engraved as a political personality into our consciousness, but his correspondence shows him to be a loving yet dispassionate friend in the lives of many. The writing he did for his newspapers is also massive.

In South Africa, he would sometimes walk 40 miles to buy things from shops because that was the closest shop. One day, he walked 55 miles. During the Zulu-Boer War, he carried an injured soldier over forty miles at a stretch. As a 44-year-old, he marched for eight days with five thousand workers over 160 miles; at the age of 61, he led a foot march at Dandi over 200 miles; at 76 years, walking in the villages of riot-torn Noakhali over three months – the man did it without tiring. In Noakhali, he walked barefoot. He did not give up in despair simply because his opponents threw trash in his path, knowing which way he would pass. At the age of 76 years, he worked for 18 hours a day and sometimes for up to 21 hours. Sometimes, one wonders what inspired him to work so hard his entire life. It is not as if he was working hard for himself.

Sometimes, the desire for power can lead to hard work, but we don't see such inspiration in Gandhi's life. On the contrary, after independence, he does not participate in the power plays; he does not even remain present in the celebrations. Independence came, partition happened, there were terrible riots in the country, and people were slaughtering each other – in such an atmosphere, the voice of 'conscience' was lost. Gandhi worked day and night trying to awaken human conscience. Why does this aged man continue doing this work in the face of humiliation, abuse and difficulties? Why? What difference would it have made if more people were left to die, even more blood spilt, and corpses could have piled up higher? It certainly did not make any difference to Sawarkar. In Noakhali, Hindus died, Hindu women were raped, but Sawarkar was not moved to go there. One can understand that Sawarkar did not go to Bihar because, over there, Muslims died in large numbers, but why did he not go to Noakhali? Gandhi could not help himself. Perhaps he could not accept that humanity was being killed before his very eyes. Perhaps it was difficult for him to see how humans were losing their conscience.

Once again, we come to the question. Why was it only Gandhi who could not bear to see this? What inspired him to push himself all life long? To jump into the midst of danger?

Gandhi was a barrister. Later, he became a leader. He was an editor, writer, journalist, printer, and everything. The question was, what was he not? It is not enough to talk about 'dignity of labour.' If such dignity is to be established, the process has to begin with oneself. Gandhi felt this, and therefore, he became a scavenger, carpenter, cobbler, ironsmith, barber, washerman, servant, cook, doctor, nurse, teacher, and weaver. He never felt ashamed of any work. This allowed him to expect the same from others.

He did all this without allowing the impish smile to leave his face. Is compassion, love, and empathy so deep in any human soul? Is this the real meaning of Sant Tukaram's *abhang' 'antariche dhave swabhave baheri* – whatever resides will emerge on its own?'

Gandhi must have been a highly interesting personality. An uninteresting personality could never have gathered people around him like bees in a honeycomb. Across the world, friends sent him gifts. Once, there was a packet of cigarettes in a gift pack for Christmas. Gandhi never smoked, so he kept the packet aside and said, "Let's keep this for Jawahar. He can smoke when he comes!" I have always felt envious about this incident.

One thing surprises me. There have been so many accusations against Gandhi that Congress never felt the need to answer these, and Gandhians, too, did not counter them effectively. Otherwise, the accusations would never have stuck with him. Now, the accusations appear so true, as if these are part of Gandhi's body and character. Why did this happen? Why does Gandhi, who is so interesting, appear so insipid? Why does his fire seem to burn so low? Did the Gandhians strangulate the activist Gandhi under the garb of constructive work through Gandhian institutions by anointing him the Father of the Nation, Mahatma Gandhi, worshipper of non-violence, follower of nonpossession, detachment, celibacy and other vows and blindly chanting Gandhi's prayers? Has Gandhi, who belonged to the Bahujans, been caged once again in the prison of elites? Have the Gandhians made Gandhi, who believed in the dignity of bread labour and who worked day and night waiting at the doorstep of parasites? Gandhi was hated by Hindutvawadis for encouraging large-scale mixing of varnas and occupations; have the Gandhians polished and smoothed him to the extent that even the Hindutvawadis could swallow him easily? Is this a conspiracy to replace Gandhi's revolutionary zeal with the '*samrasta*' of the Rashtriya Swayamsevak Sangh?

We can expect that now, on Gandhi's 150th birthday, some attention will be paid to these serious questions.

CHAPTER 15

GANDHI IS STILL ALIVE!

2nd October 2019 was the 150th birth anniversary of Gandhi. 70 years have passed since his death. Yet, one feels that Gandhi continues to live. After Gandhi's death, Vinoba was asked, "What did you think in the moment you heard of Gandhi's demise?" Upon this, Vinoba answered, "My heart felt that Gandhiji had not died, and till today, my heart feels that he is alive. Good people do not die; they remain alive, and bad people are never alive; they live in the world of imagination."

Thus, the question arises, "Why doesn't Gandhi die?"

We say that the world has changed. This might be true of technology, but is it true of the eternal spiritual values? Values such as truth, love, non-violence, and authenticity are desired by all. The world might have changed, but is there anyone who exists in the world without a desire for love and only a desire for hatred? Who is there in the world who likes it when others offer them only lies and betrayal? Who doesn't demand loyalty and truth for themselves? Who wants to die shot by a bullet? Even when I betray the world, I continue to expect loyalty. I deal falsely with the world, but I expect that the world will remain truthful towards me. I am violent, but I do not want to be the target of another's bullet. As far as I am concerned, I insist on non-violence. Even when I treat the world terribly, people should treat me well; that is my expectation. As long as these values do not die, Gandhi cannot die because, throughout his life, Gandhi has represented these values.

'You shall reap as you sow' - such is the law of nature. Will you get tomatoes if you sow eggplants? Will you get jasmine if you sow poison ivy? Impossible! Similarly, if you want love, you must sow love. If you want truth, then you must pursue it. It is here that we run into trouble with Gandhi. We want love even when we sow hatred. We want non-violence by the following violence. This is what Gandhi's terms mean and end. The means should be in accordance with the ends; this was his insistence. If you want pure ends, then you must pursue pure means; this was Gandhi's singular indication. These values, which have been at the centre of religious thought and practice, were brought into politics for the first time by Gandhi. According to him, to question the relationship between means and end is like asking why the bullock cart cannot be used to cross the ocean. If one wants to cross the ocean, then certainly the ship is the proper means, and if we insist on using the bullock cart, then we have to be prepared to touch the ocean floor along with our cart.

The prayer has to be in accordance with the deity. The relationship between means and ends is as organic as that between the seed and the plant. If we worship the devil, we should not expect the reward of praying to God. If you say, "We want to pray to god, so how does it matter if the means are devilish?" then such a statement would be of utter ignorance. As long as the natural law of you shall reap as you sow does not change till that time, there is no chance that Gandhi will die, no matter how hard one tries.

As a schoolboy, I had to wriggle out permission to watch films in a theatre. In the first place, I had to be allowed to watch a film, and then there had to be a consensus on the name of the film. Even if I could manage both permits, I still had to convince my father to sanction the budget. This was followed by a successful battle in the lines at the ticket counter. Holding a third-class ticket, I would wait for the film to start. There used to be chaos in the stalls till the film started. If a young girl appeared, there would be all kinds of comments, harassment and teasing. All this would stop as soon as the film started. On-screen, if anyone teased or harassed a young woman and the hero thrashed such a person, the audience would erupt in joyful clapping and whistles in support of the hero's actions. The audience had indulged in the same behaviour for which the villain on the screen was receiving a thrashing, and yet the viewers were all on the hero's side! If the innermost soul of the wrong-doer approves the thrashing of the wrong-doer as a 'good' act, then how can the good ever die? And as long 'good' doesn't die, no matter the age one lives, how can Gandhi be considered dead?

In every film, the basic theme revolves around the struggle between the hero and the villain, between the good and the evil and the victory of the former over the latter. It is not as if every person in the audience is virtuous; there must be a mixture of some good and some bad people, and yet why does every single person in the theatre look forward to the hero winning the battle?

It is not as if this atmosphere of excited expectation exists only in the theatres of this country. 'Harry Potter' was screened in theatres across the world, and the book was read in as many countries as possible. Harry

Potter represents good, and he fights against evil and vanquishes it. He does win on the silver screen, but why does every viewer wait with bated breath for his victory? If both the good people in the audience and the bad people support the victory of the good, then there cannot be the death of the good in any era. And because the good cannot vanquished, it does not matter how many Nathurams come and try to kill Gandhi; Gandhi cannot be vanquished. And therefore, Gandhi never dies. And therefore, it is said,

"Satya pareshan ho sakta hai, magar parachute nahi – truth can be troubled but not defeated."

Gandhi meets us at every step. We can crush under our feet the values for which Gandhi lived. And yet, we end up expecting those values in our own lives. Those who live in a world of virtue require truthful people for trade, industries and professions, but even those who live a sham life need loyal people around them; insincere professionals look for sincere colleagues, and dishonest people look for good and honest people. Therefore, one may ask, why should we lose our faith in these values of virtue, honesty, and truth, which are held dear by all good people? A thief does not employ another thief in his house, and he, too, looks for an honest man. Therefore, how can the values that Gandhi held close to his heart ever perish? And if those values remain alive, then how can Gandhi die?

Vinoba's words hold true. "Gandhi can never die, and Nathuram cannot survive."

In one poem of Kusumagraj, several great men get together and sit chatting and discussing their sorrows. One said, "I am only limited to a particular caste." Another said, "I have the same sorrow. I fought for every community, and yet I am reduced to one particular caste." Upon this, Gandhi said, "At least there is a community behind you. There is only the administrative wall behind me." Although this is Kusumagraj's poem, it expresses widely held feelings. This is the terrible reality of this country.it is not enough to have the administrative wall behind us; a caste needs to stand behind us like a wall. It is Gandhi's greatest achievement that there is no single caste that stands behind him like a wall. And yet, this is the main reason why he is made to stand as an offender. All kinds of accusations are levelled against him, and there are rare voices that are heard defending him; therefore, the accusations were presumed to be correct. The question arises of whether, if there had been a caste to stand like a wall behind him, they would have tolerated such accusations. Would the fear of retaliation reign in those who spread canards against him? Instead of seeing the pistol in Nathauram's hand as he kills Gandhi and the bullets from it tearing into the aged body, people talk about how Nathuram bowed before Gandhi before shooting, which shows that not only Nathuram's caste standing like a solid wall behind him but the Hindutvavadis and especially the Brahministic bullet-proof jacket constantly defends Nathuram. Nathuram, who is on average intellect, is made into a 'Pandit' by this wall. The womaniser Narayan Apte and effeminate Nathuram Godse are declared nationalists. How long will it take the wall standing off the foundations of falsehoods to fall? But what would happen if the falsehoods were concretised through the use of power? We are seeing it happen before our very eyes.

Gandhi belonged to everybody. A handful of people whose vested interests were challenged may have been hurt, and they hated and detested him. But the real question is, when we say that Gandhi belonged to everyone, does it mean that he belonged to no one? After all, 'everyone' is a word which does not indicate anything particular. In comparison, 'caste' appears to have real dimensions. As long as Gandhi lived, he provided 'everyone' with meaning and consciousness, but after him, the 'everyone' dissolved, and the dimesions of 'caste' became stronger. And therefore, the accusers of Gandhi became more powerful, and Gandhi-lovers lost their brightness. All his life, Gandhi worked to raise consciousness, and when that consciousness lost its rhythm, notions of caste and religion gained clout. Indeed Nathuram Godse too, makes loud assertions against Gandhi based on the strength derived from backward notions of caste and religion?

The misfortune of Gandhi is that those for whom he wore away his life do not value him. However, the freedom struggle under the leadership of Gandhi drove a perpetual wedge into the vested interests of certain elite sections who felt that pain with great intensity. This is why detractors attack him passionately, but his defenders remain apathetic. Gandhi said, 'Truth is God', but for many of us, 'convenience is truth' and 'convenience is God' as well.

In spite of everything, Gandhi did not die because even those who consider convenience as truth want the truth to be convenient because being fed lies is inconvenient for them; we all want the truth to be spoken before us. Each one of us wants to deal with truthful people. We do not want unfaithful, disloyal people to surround us. Each one of us wants loyalty, and as long this situation remains unchanged, till then Gandhi will not die.

Till then Gandhi remains immortal.